W9-CAO-938

INSTITUTE OF LEADERSHIP & MANAGEMENT **ilm**

SUPERSERIES

Managing
Relationships
Work

FOURTH EDITION

Published for the
Institute of Leadership & Management by

Pergamon
Flexible
Learning

OXFORD   AMSTERDAM   BOSTON   LONDON   NEW YORK   PARIS
SAN DIEGO   SAN FRANCISCO   SINGAPORE   SYDNEY   TOKYO

Pergamon Flexible Learning
An imprint of Elsevier Science
Linacre House, Jordan Hill, Oxford OX2 8DP
200 Wheeler Road, Burlington, MA 01803

First published 1986
Second edition 1991
Third edition 1997
Fourth edition 2003

British Library Cataloguing in Publication Data
A catalogue record for this book is available from the British Library

ISBN 0 7506 5891 6

For information on Pergamon Flexible Learning
visit our website at www.bh.com/pergamonfl

Institute of Leadership & Management
registered office
1 Giltspur Street
London
EC1A 9DD
Telephone 020 7294 3053
www.i-l-m.com
ILM is part of the City & Guilds Group

The views expressed in this work are those of the authors and do
not necessarily reflect those of the Institute of Leadership &
Management or of the publisher

Author: Dela Jenkins
Editor: Dela Jenkins
Partly based on previous material by: Elaine Horrocks, Joe Johnson,
Howard Senter and Diana Thomas
Editorial management: Genesys, www.genesys-consultants.com
Composition by Genesis Typesetting Limited, Rochester, Kent
Printed and bound in Great Britain by MPG Books, Bodmin

Contents

Workbook introduction

1 ILM Super Series study links

This workbook addresses the issues of *Managing Relationships at Work*. Should you wish to extend your study to other Super Series workbooks covering related or different subject areas, you will find a comprehensive list at the back of this book.

2 Links to ILM Qualifications

This workbook relates to the following learning outcomes in segments from the ILM Level 3 Introductory Certificate in First Line Management and the Level 3 Certificate in First Line Management.

C2.5 Interpersonal Skills/Trust
1 Appreciate the importance of effective working relationships
2 Understand the changing nature of relationships in the workplace
3 Demonstrate respect for the needs of others through your working practices
4 Act positively to build trust within working relationships
5 Respect confidentiality in the workplace

C2.7 Influencing and Negotiation
1 Explain and apply the principles of negotiation
2 Recognize the importance of non-verbal communication and social skills in effective negotiation
3 Influence people to achieve identified objectives
4 Reduce resistance and minimize conflict
5 Know when and how to accept the opinions, values and will of others
6 Work to achieve a win-win situation

3 Links to S/NVQs in Management

This workbook relates to the following elements of the Management Standards, which are used in S/NVQs in Management, as well as a range of other S/NVQs.

C1.1 Develop your skills to improve your performance;
C4.1 Gain the trust and support of colleagues and team members;
C4.3 Minimise confict in your team;
C9.1 Contribute to the identification of development needs.

It will also help you to develop the following Personal Competences:

- acting assertively;
- communicating;
- managing self;
- influencing others.

4 Workbook objectives

What do you recall about past jobs you have done and places you have worked in? Almost inevitably, the memories will be about feelings – what you enjoyed, who you liked working with, what made the job satisfying, how you felt when you left.

The purpose of this workbook is to look at feelings and relationships at work. You will learn about the dynamics of team relationships and how you can develop interpersonal skills which will make you a truly effective first line manager.

In Session A we consider the 'external' relationships between people in organizations – including management structures and the effect of organization structure.

Session B discusses the importance of group harmony and the steps you can take to make a group feel like a cohesive team. It goes on to describe the personal qualities and interpersonal skills you will need to lead the team to its full potential.

Session C concentrates on the skills of influencing, persuading and negotiation. It considers the influences which have an impact on parties to negotiations, and the techniques you can use in order to persuade people to reach a compromise. It ends by discussing those skills that are particularly relevant to the art of negotiation.

Finally, in Session D we look at conflict in the workplace. Nearly all conflicts involve underlying emotional issues. The stronger the feelings, the more difficult the resolution. To resolve conflicts it is essential to address the feelings of all parties. We will consider a conflict resolution model, which you can use to discover the true causes of conflict within your team, and which will enable you to choose the best option to achieve a win-win solution.

4.1 Objectives

When you have completed this workbook you will be better able to:

- describe the types of structure which form the basis of relationships in organizations;
- develop qualities and skills that will promote positive team relationships;
- apply the principles of influence and persuasion to achieve objectives;
- use appropriate techniques to resolve conflict.

5 Activity planner

Activity 3 requires you to obtain an organization chart showing the relationship of authority between the managers in your department

Activity 18, Activity 24 and Activity 46 may provide the basis of evidence for your S/NVQ portfolio. All Portfolio Activities and the Work-based assignment are sign-posted with this icon.

The icon states the elements to which the Portfolio Activities and Work-based assignment relate.

The Work-based assignment (on page 106) will require that you spend time gathering information and talking to colleagues and people in your workteam. You might like to start thinking about whom you should approach, and perhaps arrange a time to chat with them. The assignment should be useful in helping to demonstrate your competence in:

- acting assertively;
- communicating;
- managing self;
- influencing others.

Session A
The importance of good relationships

1 Introduction

Every organization is a complex combination of land, buildings, machinery, intellectual property, systems, cultures and, above all, people. The people form a complex organism – rather like a hive of bees – with each person interacting with all the others to a greater or lesser extent, and each making its own contribution to the good of the whole.

This session looks at the ways in which the members of the organization – the bees – interrelate, and the nature of their relationship.

2 A definition of 'relationship'

What precisely do we mean by the word 'relationship'? If you consult a thesaurus, you will come up with related terms such as 'alliance', 'connection' and 'dependence'. So obviously it is some sort of close association between people.

In any organization the nature of that association (or relationship) depends on the structure of the organization and its culture. In small organizations the relationships between people are often relatively straightforward. In large organizations they can be far more complex.

Activity 1

3 mins

Imagine that you work in a large organization (which may be the case anyway). Tick all those people in the organization with whom you think you would have a relationship.

Managing director	☐
Directors	☐
Senior managers	☐
Line managers	☐
Section or department heads	☐
Team leaders	☐
Senior employees	☐
Junior employees	☐

You will probably have found that, after some thought, you ticked everyone on the list because, as you will learn later in this workbook, everyone in an organization has the power to influence others, and therefore can be said to have a relationship with them.

3 Formal and informal relationships within organizations

In modern organizations there is a whole variety of relationship structures, ranging from formal, relatively static ones with a defined line of command to fluid ones that are constantly evolving to meet the needs of the business.

We will look briefly at the following four examples of formal relationships within an organisation:

- line relationships;
- staff relationships;
- functional relationships;
- matrix relationships.

3.1 Line relationships

In a line relationship each person below the person at the top has one boss and only one boss. Thus a job holder in one position has the power and authority to direct and manage the work of those below who are on the same line.

This establishes a chain of command or line of control from the top of the organization to the bottom. Organization charts are often used to show line relationships and you will probably be familiar with these from work or your other studies. An example of an organization chart for a social services department is shown below.

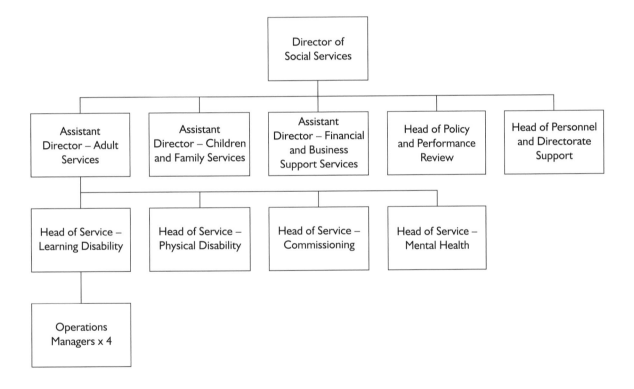

Activity 2

2 mins

Do organization charts:

a tell you anything about the people who hold the jobs?   Yes/No

b indicate precisely what the responsibilities of the job
   holders are?   Yes/No

c give any idea of the power held by one person compared
   to another in the same or another department?   Yes/No

You have probably realised that organisation charts tell you nothing about the people who hold the jobs or their precise responsibilities. However, they do give some idea of the power people hold as a result of their position in the department and the people they report to. This is known as 'position power'.

So an organization chart tells you the relative degree of power that goes with each job, i.e. how high up the organization the job position is. The higher in the chart, the more power and authority.

The line relationship is found in many organizations, but the move in the last decade or so to flatter organization structures diminishes this form of power. In flat organizations, first line managers carry a very substantial management responsibility.

> The armed forces are a good example of organizations with a strong chain of command. Everyone knows their place. Position power is backed up by strict disciplinary procedures.

Activity 3

20 mins

Obtain a copy of the organization chart for your department. Your line manager should have one. Find out how up-to-date it is, who uses it and for what purpose. Does it really reflect the way power is exercised in your organization?

3.2 Staff relationships

Look at this extract from an organization chart of a production department.

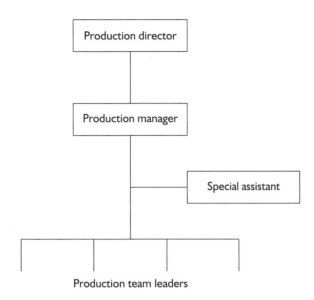

A special assistant, such as the one on the right in the chart, is a 'staff officer' whose job is to act in an advisory capacity in the name of the manager. Part of the role will involve liaising with team members and giving advice during decision making. The relationship between the staff officer and others reporting to the manager is called a staff relationship.

Activity 4   2 mins

Use the extract organization chart above to answer the following questions.

a Does the assistant have power over the production team
   leaders?   Yes/No

b Do the team leaders have power over the assistant?   Yes/No

No doubt you realised that there is no direct line of control connecting the two. So the answer to both questions is 'No'. Neither has power over the other. The team leaders use the assistant as a source of information and advice but don't take instructions from him or her. They would still be able to go to their manager directly if a problem arose.

3.3 Functional relationships

Functional relationships exist between line managers and functional specialists (those people who carry out specific functions to support the activities of the rest of the organization). Some examples of functional specialists are:

- human resource officers;
- accountants;
- health and safety officers;
- members of the legal department.

In most organizations the human resources department acts in a functional relationship with other departments. It has no power over other departments except when it comes to recruitment, interpretation of employment law and other personnel matters.

3.4 Matrix relationships

It is becoming more common nowadays for employees to work for more than one boss. One possible arrangement is a matrix relationship, shown in the chart opposite.

The project managers in the chart report to the production manager for both administrative purposes and work direction (so it is a line relationship). However, the situation is different for the three team leaders. All three report to the production manager for administration purposes. However, team leaders 1 and 2 both work on the project run by project manager A, to whom they report for work direction, while team leader 3 works on the project run by project manager B and reports to this manager for work direction.

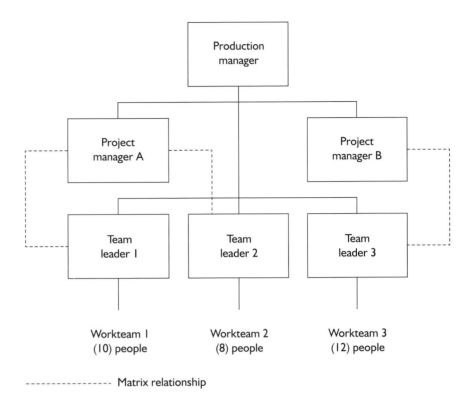

Workteam 1 (10) people Workteam 2 (8) people Workteam 3 (12) people

------------- Matrix relationship

Activity 5

3 mins

Answer the following questions relating to the above case.

1 How many managers does each of the team leaders report to?

2 How many people report to the production manager?

You should have seen that the team leaders each report to two managers. Five people report to the production manager.

3.5 Informal relationships

On the organization charts we have looked at, you will probably have noticed that there are no lines running between departments and teams. This is misleading because it suggests that there are no links between them.

From your own experience you know that there is a great deal of communication between all levels within an organization. This is often in the form of informal relationships, but these are never shown on any chart. The reason for this is simply that informal relationships between people in an organization are so numerous that a chart of them would be too complex to be comprehensible.

In larger organizations many of the informal relationships we build internally will be through joining formal or informal groups connected to social activities, or by getting to know people when attending meetings relating to our work role.

Activity 6

5 mins

Make a list of the opportunities that have enabled you to make informal contacts in your organization.

_____

_____

_____

You may have mentioned membership of sports clubs, social clubs, trades unions, and perhaps attendance at such regular events as monthly management meetings, production meetings, safety committee, staff association committee and quality circle meetings.

These informal contacts are invaluable in creating a support network to help you in your work. You can learn more about developing informal networks in the workbook *Networking and Sharing Information* in this series.

4 External relationships

During your everyday job you may sometimes come into contact with people from another department or from outside the organization who have an impact on how you carry out your role.

Activity 7

3 mins

Over the last six months what external contacts have you made during your everyday work activities?

_____

_____

_____

_____

You could have mentioned a whole host of contacts, including suppliers, customers, auditors, contractors and specialist consultants.

4.1 Specialist consultants

In the last few years it has become very common for external experts to be brought in on a short-term basis to advise on a particular problem or project. Examples would be management consultants and IT specialists.

It is not always easy to know how to liaise with external experts brought in to work with your team. The lines of authority can be blurred and other members of the team may find it difficult to accept and implement their proposals.

Activity 8 · 3 mins

Suppose that your team is involved in setting up a new computer system for one of its existing projects. Your manager calls in a computer expert from an external consultancy firm. How should you interact with this expert? Tick the box(es) that seem correct.

Accept everything the expert has to say and don't ask questions, after all they are being paid to give advice. ☐

Be positive and willing to learn, but don't let you own authority be overridden. ☐

Encourage your team members to ask common sense questions and request clarification where things aren't clear to them. ☐

Test the logic and practicality of what the expert proposes. ☐

Correct any misunderstandings of tasks under discussion. ☐

You could tick every item except the first. When you are dealing with an expert (whether internal or external) everyone benefits if you and your team members feel free to ask common sense questions – it's the best way of preventing misunderstandings arising on either side. And by all means test the logic and practicality of what is being proposed. After all, while the experts know all they need to know about their expert subject, they will probably know very little about your work environment and the way your systems and team function.

You should aim to build a relationship of mutual help and trust between you, your team and the external expert. This will improve your personal power, ensure the commitment of everyone involved, and help to achieve the team's overall work objectives.

5 Differences between people – the effects on relationship building

Towards the end of the Second World War, Dr Eric Berne was responsible for signing the discharge papers of thousands of American sailors. One of his duties was to decide whether each of them was of 'sound mind'. Years later he used his experiences to develop a theory, now known as **transactional analysis** (TA), which is used today by psychoanalysts to shed light on the way people feel and behave.

The theory is that our experiences as children leave an indelible impression on us, and the feelings we have during that period of our lives have a strong influence on our current behaviour. TA is a simple and practical way of understanding and modifying that behaviour.

According to Berne, everyone's mode of behaviour can be classified into one of three groups, or 'ego-states', which he named:

- Parent;
- Adult;
- Child.

Each ego-state has its own characteristics.

5.1 Parent

Parent behaviour is typified by feelings of what is right and wrong. People with dominant Parent ego-states have a strong sense of protection and discipline. They are dogmatic and have controlling personalities.

Parent behaviour is divided into two sub groups:

- Critical Parent – whose behaviour is typically moralising, critical, prejudiced and authoritarian.
- Nurturing Parent – who is sympathetic, comforting and protective.

People dealing with them may feel that they are being treated like children; this can be annoying for some, comforting for others.

5.2 Adult

Adult behaviour involves gathering information, evaluating it and using it to make and carry out decisions. It is different from the other two ego-states in that it involves thinking rather than feeling. 'Adults' are typically logical, rational, calculating and unemotional. Others may see them as fair and balanced or as cold, distant and even unsympathetic.

5.3 Child

Child behaviour is spontaneous, controlled by strong feelings of either joy or sorrow.

Child behaviour is divided into three sub-groups.

■ Natural Child – who is typically fun-loving, emotional, irresponsible and innocent.
■ Adapted Child – a version of Natural Child, which has been toned down to be more acceptable to other people.
■ Manipulative Child – whose behaviour is sly, creative and cute.

Such people can be perceived by others as immature, irresponsible, irritating, childish or, at the other extreme, loveable and innocent.

While we are all likely to display all three behaviours at some time or other, the behaviour of every one of us is dominated by one ego-state in particular. However, we can change or adapt any one of them if the circumstances are right.

5.4 How transactional analysis works

Berne represented the communication between people as a 'transaction'. One person sends out a message (or 'stimulus') and the other person responds to it (the 'response').

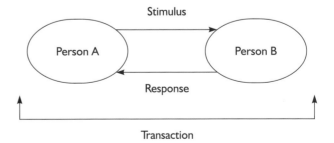

The way in which Person A responds to the stimulus sent from Person B will depend very much on the ego-state of each party.

Transactions can be either 'complementary' or 'crossed'. If they are complementary, then the stimulus sent by Person A will get the expected response from Person B, and both sides will feel on the same wave length.

On the other hand, if a transaction is crossed, then the stimulus from Person A will be met by an unexpected response from Person B, and the message will not get across in the way Person A intends, i.e. the 'wires will be crossed'.

This can be shown in the following diagrams. Each circle represents a person who is behaving predominantly as a Parent, Adult or Child. The arrows represent messages sent between two of them.

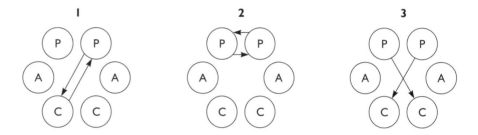

In diagram 1, one of the people acting like a Parent is sending a stimulus to a person acting like a Child. The Parent's dominating behaviour is complementary to the Child's irresponsible behaviour, so the wires are not 'crossed' and the message will be received in the way the Parent intended.

In diagram 2, again the transaction is complementary (Parent to Parent), so the stimulus will be met by the expected response, and the two parties will be on the same wave length.

In diagram 3 the parties have problems. Here both are acting like Parents, and are expecting a response to their message from someone acting like a Child. However, the message they get back is from another Parent, with the result that the wires are crossed. There will be no 'meeting of minds' here. For example, the first person acting as a Parent could be saying: 'That isn't the right way to open the till' while the second person (also acting like a Parent) could respond: 'I know exactly what I am doing, thank you'.

Activity 9 · *3 mins*

Below are three transactions between team members who have dominant ego-states as either Parents, Adults or Children. Draw a line between each transaction and the diagram which represents it. For example, if you think that the middle diagram represents the people taking part in Transaction 1, draw a line between the diagram and the transaction.

Transaction 1	Transaction 2	Transaction 3
Stimulus: 'Do you know what time the meeting starts?' *Response*: 'How should I know? No-one ever tells me anything!'	*Stimulus*: 'Oh, dear! The printer won't work.' *Response*: 'Well I don't know how to do it.'	*Stimulus*: 'Let's see if we can drink eight pints before closing time.' *Response*: Great idea!

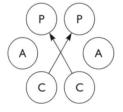 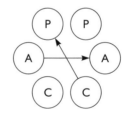 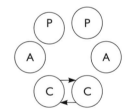

You will find the answers on page 117.

5.5 The value of transactional analysis

EXTENSION 1

An excellent explanation of transactional analysis can be found in Peter Honey's book *Improve your People Skills*.

An understanding of the principles of TA can help you to manage the relationships between you and your team and between different members of the team.

Thus, while each of us habitually behaves in a particular way (i.e. Parent, Adult or Child), our habitual feelings can be controlled and, if necessary, replaced by more appropriate ones. For example, we can be helped to replace negative feelings of indecision or rebellion (Child), or criticism (Parent) with more positive (Adult) ones.

By understanding the principles of TA, and learning to recognise the habitual behaviours in your team, you can help them to change their unproductive behaviours, to uncross their wires and improve communication and understanding.

Dave has always been a difficult sort of chap. If anything goes wrong with the code he is checking, he will become agitated and say he can't cope with so much pressure. His team leader, Rachel, has never known quite how to handle Dave's outbursts, and they have usually ended up ignoring each other for hours. But, after attending a course on transactional analysis, she decides to try a new approach.

Dave obviously has a Child ego-state. Rachel decides to respond as a Parent to his outburst by saying lightheartedly 'Now hang on, Dave, it's not the end of the world!'. This makes the transaction complementary. She can then try to move him from the Child ego-state to Adult, for example by asking for his opinion or asking how he thinks the pressure on him might be reduced.

By learning how to recognize Dave's habitual behaviour pattern (ego-state) Rachel can respond to it in a complementary way, and then try to change it to a more satisfactory one.

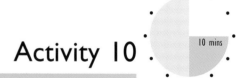

Activity 10

Think about the members of your team. Use the table below to classify them according to their dominant ego-states. Remember, most people have more than one ego-state, but one of them will be dominant.

Team member	Parent	Adult	Child

15

6 Relationships and organizational culture

6.1 What do we mean by 'organizational culture'?

Organizational culture is the easiest thing to recognize and at the same time the most difficult thing to define.

One popular definition is that it is 'a system of shared meaning held by members of the organization that distinguishes it from other organizations'.

The 'shared meaning' could be about, for example, what it means to be an employee of that organization, or why the organization exists.

The type of relationship between people in an organization strongly reflects the culture of that organization. For example, relationships in one of the armed forces could be very different from, say, a charity. The first is highly structured, with strict codes of conduct, a rigid hierarchy and a highly directive leadership style. The charity would typically be much more collaborative, have a less hierarchical structure and, since it relies to a large extent on voluntary labour, would be very people-oriented.

6.2 Differences in organizational culture, and the effects on relationship building at work

One way in which organizational culture can be classified is according to the organization's orientation. There are at least three types:

- profit-oriented;
- system-oriented;
- people-oriented.

The priorities of the organization are established according to its orientation. For example, in a highly profit-oriented company, profit will be considered to be more important than everything else, and its systems and people will be managed in a way that supports the priority of profit. In contrast, the armed forces are system-oriented, and their systems and people will be managed in ways that support the overall strategy of the organization in either peace or war.

To learn more about organizational culture, you may like to see *Organizational Culture and Context* in this series.

The significance for you is that the organization's culture determines the quality of support you receive from higher management levels in your attempts to build strong team relationships – and the way you go about building those relationships.

A profit-oriented company, which puts little value on its people, is likely to have low morale and a high staff turnover. On the other hand, a people-oriented company (such as Hewlett Packard in the 1980s and 1990s) will put great emphasis on keeping both its staff and customers happy, even if this means that short-term profits may be reduced.

Self-assessment 1

12 mins

1 Draw a line to link each of the descriptions in the right-hand column with its correct name in the left-hand column.

Matrix relationships	Where each person has one manager and there is a chain of command or line of control from the top of the organization to the bottom.
Line relationships	Where a specially appointed staff officer acts in an advisory capacity in the name of the manager and works closely with the team members.
Functional relationships	How specialists, who have authority in certain areas only, relate to the line managers and team leaders.
Staff relationships	Where a manager or team leader reports to two or more senior managers for different purposes.

2 Suggest two ways in which you can develop informal relationships at work.

3 What problems might you encounter in liaising with external experts?

4 What are the three ego-states in transactional analysis?

5 An understanding of the principles of _____ _____ can help you to manage the _____ between you and your team and between different members of the team.

6 Write the behaviours listed below in the correct ego-state boxes.

Parent	Adult	Child

Protective	Spontaneous	Unemotional	Fun-loving
Calculating	Authoritarian	Manipulative	Critical

Answers to these questions can be found on page 114.

7 Summary

- Line relationships exist where there is a defined chain of command from the top of an organization to the bottom.

- Staff relationships hinge on a specially appointed staff officer who acts in an advisory capacity in the name of the manager and works closely with team members.

- Functional relationships describe the arrangement in which functional specialists who have authority in certain areas only, such as accountants and human resource specialists, relate to line managers.

- Matrix relationships exist where a manager or team leader reports to two (or possibly more) bosses for different purposes.

- Informal relationships are a very important means of communication but they aren't recorded on organization charts.

- When dealing with an external expert, you need to develop a culture of trust and co-operation between you, the expert and your team.

- According to transactional analysis (TA) everyone's mode of behaviour can be classified into three groups, or 'ego-states':
  - Parent;
  - Adult;
  - Child.

- You can use the principles of TA to help your team to change their unproductive behaviours, to uncross their wires and improve communication and understanding.

- Organizational culture can be classified into at least three types, depending on the organization's priorities. The types are profit-oriented, system-oriented or people-oriented.

Session B
Building a positive environment

1 Introduction

Your position as a first line manager gives you all the formal position power needed to carry out your leadership role. However, there is much more to leading a really successful team than simply having the necessary positional power. To lead a successful team you need 'personal power'.

Personal power is more than just 'charisma'. It is derived from the personal qualities and interpersonal skills you gain when learning to be a good manager.

In this part of the workbook we will look at personal power and the social skills and competencies you need in order to build a strong, united team that has a culture of loyalty and trust. But, first, we need to understand what we mean by a 'team'.

2 Groups and teams

In his classic book *The New Manager* (1994) Mike Woods says that people in a work environment have three kinds of need for human contact. The three categories are as follows.

- Joining and belonging – the need for group contact.
- Role and control – the need to have a clear role or control of others.
- Pairing and sharing – the need for individual contacts on a one-to-one basis.

21

EXTENSION 2
The New Manager by
Mike Woods is an
invaluable guide to
improving the skills of
people management for
the new manager.

According to Woods, the amount of human contact we require varies from individual to individual but, whenever people are put together, they become subject to group dynamics. In any group there will be a mixture of people with different kinds of need. Some will have a strong need to belong, while others will need to control and yet others will have strong sharing needs. All these needs have to be met before the group can function effectively as a team. And it is part of your role as first line manager to develop skills that will enable you to fulfil these needs and turn the group of people within your area of responsibility into a team.

A team is a very particular type of group. When you became a first line manager you may have experienced the people you managed as rather a random group.

2.1 The dynamics of a group

This story was told to me by an old man who was brought up in Poland during the 1930s. It tells us something interesting about group dynamics.

'When I was a small child – seven or eight – I was often sent to get the cows in for milking. I used to ask myself: "How come a small boy with a stick can make these 20 big cows do what he wants?" Later I realized. Each cow looked around and thought – "I'm up against 19 cows and a small boy. I'd better play it safe".'

This doesn't mean that people in groups behave like a herd of cows. Human beings are conscious and have will power; they can discuss, argue and object. However, it is generally accepted that membership of a group does affect the behaviour of individuals in a number of ways.

- Individuals in groups may feel isolated and lacking in confidence.
- They may feel it is 'safer' to go with the majority.
- This can tend to reinforce the confidence of the majority . . .
- . . . which in turn can give the individuals confidence to do and say things they would not otherwise do and say.

This means that:

- a single strong personality can sometimes influence a group in a particular direction;
- an organized minority within a group of people who don't know each other can often determine the group's attitude and actions;
- the attitudes and intentions of such random groups can be quite unstable, and can swing first one way and then the other.

Activity 11

2 mins

Which of the following statements points to the best strategy for a person wishing to influence a group?

- Take a firm line, try to dominate and, if necessary, intimidate the group.
- Start by convincing one or two members of the group and use them to influence the rest.
- Watch carefully for reactions and modify your approach in the light of these.

You would be right to say that the third statement describes the most useful approach. It is highly unwise to try to intimidate a group. They can easily react against you, and it isn't necessarily easy to sway a group from the outside. One obvious factor about a more or less random group is that they are strangers: an outsider doesn't know them any more than they know each other. For this reason the second statement is also the wrong choice – you don't know enough about the members of a group to identify the 'opinion formers'. This approach can however work with a team, as we will see in Session C.

Only by paying careful attention to reactions can a speaker tell what the members of a random group feel and which way they are capable of moving. It takes a great deal of skill and experience to communicate effectively with random groups.

In practice few groups that you encounter at work are likely to be truly random. In most cases they will work for you and will share at least some of your attitudes, values and enthusiasms.

2.2 How do teams differ from groups?

There are some important distinctions between a group and a team. The following example sums them up neatly.

Activity 12

4 mins

'As the busker began to play, a handful of passers-by stopped to listen.'

We can think of these listeners as a group, but all they had in common was the fact that they happened to be passing by when the busker began to play. Apart from this they may well have been complete strangers.

So how would you say a team differs from a group?

_____

_____

_____

_____

There is a strong clue in the way we asked the question. The members of a group may have little in common. The members of a team, by contrast, have – or should have – a lot in common.

The people who form a work team are expected to:

- know each other
  - they will understand each others' abilities and interests, strengths and weaknesses, and will be comfortable in each others' company;
  - they may well have social contact outside work;

- share values and goals
  - they will work together to achieve common objectives;
  - they will tend to have similar attitudes towards the organization, the job, the team leader and people outside the team;

- possess a sense of common identity and team spirit
  - they will support one another;
  - they will work flexibly, exchanging roles and tasks when appropriate.

  Some teams are more developed than others, but a team is clearly a very different organism from a group.

2.3 What makes a strong team?

Teams play a very important role in modern organizations. One of your roles as a first line manager will include building a strong, effective team. To do this you need to help team members to:

■ understand each others' roles and specific tasks;
■ understand the team objectives and how team members can work together to achieve them;
■ discuss problems as they arise;
■ work together to implement decisions.

Most effective teams are made up of at least five roles, each with its own responsibilities and strengths. It is your job to match the people in your team to these roles according to their individual attributes and skills. The diagram below shows one way in which these roles can be categorised.

EXTENSION 1
Peter Honey's book,
Improve Your People Skills,
has many useful tips on
how to build successful
teams.

The characteristics of each role are as follows.

Role	Characteristics
Achiever	Encourages the team to get on with the current task.
Provocateur	Gets the team to look more critically at what they are doing, and tries to improve on it.
Consolidator	Encourages everyone to work together to achieve clearly expressed objectives.
Reflector	Produces new, well-considered ideas and evaluates the ideas of other members of the team.
Mediator	Helps to keep a harmonious atmosphere and resolves conflict within the team.

Very often there is an additional role of Specialist who is outside the team itself, but who is there as a resource for the team members to call on as necessary.

Care in selecting team members for the different roles will certainly pay off in increased efficiency and effectiveness. Some team members, for example, may be very good at getting the job done but not particularly good at relating to people. Such people will play the provocateur role. Other team members may be full of ideas but not very effective at implementing these ideas or completing allocated tasks. These will be reflectors.

Activity 13

Think about the members of your team. Which of the team roles listed above do you think they normally play? And which would they be best suited for? (Bear in mind that they might be perfectly suited to the roles that they currently occupy.)

Team member	Current role	Most appropriate role

Once you have identified the best role for each member of your team, you will need to decide what steps you will take to move them into those roles (unless they hold them already). If there are any role gaps (for example, you may not have anyone who is obviously skilled at being a reflector), is there anyone who could be trained to take on that role?

Self-managing teams are a relatively recent alternative to the traditional hierarchy (where there was a chain of command from the top to the bottom of an organization). This new structure is more challenging in that it allows the team to take responsibility for day-to-day operations. But such a team will only be really effective if you, as the first line manager, are able to:

■ allocate the team members to the roles that best suit their skills and competencies;
■ develop an atmosphere of trust, respect and mutual support within the team.

We have already looked at the allocation of roles. The rest of this section considers the ways in which you can encourage behaviours in your team that build trust, respect and mutual support.

3 Behaviour breeds behaviour

3.1 The power of behaviour

Your behaviour is important because it may be the only visible indication of your real self – your hidden thoughts, motives and feelings.

> Gordon Spink had been the life and soul of the *Yorkshire Lass Inn* for years. Every night he would buy a round for anyone he didn't know, and then regale them, and anyone else prepared to listen, with his memories of life as a fighter pilot. By the time he died, he had become one of the most celebrated characters in the village, and everyone waited for the fly-past which he had always bragged would be given in his honour when he finally met his maker. Imagine their wonder when it was revealed that he had never been further than a day trip to Calais in a Cessna light aircraft, and that his working years had been spent at the controls of a JCB rather than those of a fighter 'plane.

The only clues as to Gordon's real life and history had been his flamboyant lifestyle and claims of glory. People could only judge him by what they saw and heard.

The way you behave is important because:

- your behaviour may be the only means that people have of judging you;
- the way you behave influences how other people behave (behaviour breeds behaviour);
- you can modify other people's behaviour through changing your own behaviour (remember transactional analysis).

3.2 Your behaviour and leadership skills

As a first line manager you need to develop your own patterns of behaviour so that similar desirable patterns will be inspired in your team. These patterns of behaviour will be the foundation of your personal power.

So how do you do it? What social skills do you need to acquire if you are going change the behaviour of your team members by your example?

Activity 14

6 mins

Think of a manager you really admire. It may be someone with whom you work now or have known in the past. Think about how they behave.

What words would you use to describe their personal 'qualities', i.e. their values and beliefs? For example, you might say that they value honesty or that they believe in fair play.

_____

_____

_____

And what characteristics (interpersonal skills) make them so good at interacting with other people? For example, you might say that they show that they are interested in other people, or that they have a great sense of humour.

_____

_____

_____

You may have mentioned some of the following personal qualities and interpersonal skills.

Personal qualities	Interpersonal skills
Loyalty Dependability Integrity Fairness Determination	Ability to inspire Openness Empathy Firmness Flexibility Humour Interest in others

Together these factors make up an overall pattern of behaviour that will contribute to being a good leader.

4 Personal qualities

The way your team behaves depends very much on the way you behave, and you can hardly expect them to be honest, dependable and loyal unless you are the same.

Let's take a look at some of the personal qualities and behaviours needed by a good first line manager.

4.1 Loyalty

Activity 15

12 mins

Martin Sellars leads a team of part-time paid employees and voluntary workers for a large regional charity for the physically disabled. At the monthly management meeting Martin is under fire. The regional director, Frances Dawes, says 'Martin, I have a few concerns about whether your team is delivering the service levels that our clients want. We've had quite a few complaints about your staff not turning up at clients' houses when they've been promised a visit. Is there a problem?'

Martin replies 'My problem is that I've got more volunteers in my team than anyone else. A lot of them aren't properly trained and they often don't turn up for work when I expect them to. It's all very well for Jan, Ravinda and Dave to look so complacent. They've got more paid staff and the pick of the volunteers. If you'd give me a decent team I'd soon show you what I could do.'

Answer the following questions about the above incident.

How do you think Frances will react to Martin's words?

_____

_____

If reports of what Martin has said at the meeting get back to his team, how do you think they will react?

_____

_____

From what you've heard, do you think Martin is likely to do better with a different team?

_____

_____

Martin has shown himself to be a very poor people manager. He doesn't seem to realize that voluntary workers usually need lots of encouragement and support when working in a team with paid employees. The lack of training for volunteers is also a worrying sign of Martin not valuing their contribution to the team.

Frances isn't likely to be impressed and may be thinking that she's made a mistake by appointing Martin to a managerial position in the first place.

If Martin's team hear about his comments, their morale will almost certainly drop. Their performance certainly won't improve and many of the volunteers may decide to leave.

Martin is unlikely to fare better with another team unless he changes his attitude. He doesn't seem to have the personal competencies of team building and relating to and showing sensitivity to others. This small incident could have a major impact on the team. It emphasizes the point that managers who want loyalty from the team must be loyal in return.

4.2 Dependability

Dependability obviously means doing what you have said you will do. This might be in relation to something specific such as 'I will let you have the database entries by Monday lunchtime', or it might be something more wide-ranging to do with the reliability and consistency with which you carry out your job.

Being dependable means that you will put yourself out to meet commitments you have given, and that you are prepared to give someone else's objectives a high priority. But developing a reputation for dependability isn't something you can achieve overnight. Being dependable means that you can be relied upon and will come up with the goods every time. That implies that you demonstrate dependability over and over again.

'Coming up with the goods' cannot just be a question of driving yourself and your team harder and harder to meet other people's deadlines, though this is a situation which you can easily fall into if it is taken for granted that you can be relied upon in any circumstances. Being dependable means being realistic about what you can and cannot achieve and making that position clear. Unrealistic promises about what you can deliver, or regularly giving in to pressure to meet unrealistic demands, will inevitably lead to failure sooner or later, and there goes your reputation for dependability. This is not to say that you should be negative or pessimistic in discussions, but the dependable manager usually brings some cool realism to discussions about what can be done. In fact it is often better to overestimate the time needed to complete a task and then finish it early rather than to underestimate it and finish late.

4.3 Integrity

It is also important for a first line manager to show integrity. This means you should stick to your principles and be honest and consistent. Managers who show integrity get respect.

Activity 16 · 1 min

Manager Dougal blows hot and cold. Most of the time he is lax about discipline, but every now and then he clamps down hard. He urges his team to be honest while being devious himself. He tries to take short cuts to get results and tells his boss one thing while doing another.

The people in Manager Lenny's team always know what to expect. He sets himself high standards and expects his team members to do the same. He tries to be honest and straightforward with the team and in his dealings with his boss. He is firm but fair.

Which manager would you rather work for?

Dougal ☐   Lenny ☐

Most people would probably prefer to work for Lenny. The difference between them is that Lenny is consistent and honest and sticks to his principles, while Dougal isn't and doesn't. Lenny has the personal competencies of commitment to excellence and an ethical perspective.

4.4 Fairness

Activity 17 · 3 mins

You are a first line manager in a small light engineering company. Two members of your workteam want some time off. Jennifer is a good worker, is always on time and rarely asks for time off. Pauline, however, frequently asks for time off and is quite fond of taking the odd day off without permission.

You decide that you could afford one being away but not both.

a Which one should you give the time off to?

Jennifer ☐   Pauline ☐

b On what grounds?

_____

_____

_____

_____

Your inclination may be to give time off to Jennifer, as she rarely takes time off and so is the more deserving case. This seems reasonable and fair.

However, you may argue that you may as well let Pauline have the time off because she'll probably take it anyway. This would be a decision based on expediency, not fairness.

Your responsibility must lie with the team as a whole. When trying to decide actions of this kind, you need to ask yourself: 'If I do this, what will be the effect on the whole team and on the task the team is performing?'

You can't expect everyone to always agree with your decisions, but you need to exercise the personal competence of judgement in these situations. Try to be fair and always explain your reasons to your team members so that you are also **seen** to be fair. This is seldom easy. Perhaps the secret is getting to know your team members really well so that there's mutual trust between you. (You will find tips on how to do this in section 7 of this session.)

4.5 Determination

It is very unlikely that all your decisions at work will turn out to be correct all the time. Like everybody else, first line managers sometimes make mistakes. But you can correct most wrong decisions. Just because you aren't always right doesn't mean that you and your team won't be successful.

Success in team leadership depends upon determination as much as anything else. If you show that you have the persistence to do better and overcome problems then this is one of the best ways to inspire your team.

Activity 18 · 15 mins

S/NVQ C1.1

This Activity will help you to review what you have learned so far about personal qualities. It could provide the basis of appropriate evidence for your S/NVQ portfolio. If you are intending to take this course of action, it might be better to write your answers on separate sheets of paper.

a In the following table tick the personal qualities that currently contribute to your management style. Identify any weaknesses and, in the 'Action planned' column, suggest further action to improve these areas. You may like to copy out the table onto a separate sheet of paper.

Analysis of personal qualities

Personal quality	Well developed	Good but could be improved	Inadequate	Action planned
Loyalty				
Dependability				
Integrity				
Fairness				
Determination				

b Think of an occasion in the recent past when you have had to reduce tension between members of your staff and encourage them to focus on the team's main task.

Explain how application of your personal qualities contributed to the success of the situation. Could your handling of it have been improved by an enhancement of these personal qualities? Give specific details.

_____

_____

_____

_____

_____

_____

You could add to this activity by asking someone else in the team to carry out the same analysis of your performance in your role of first line manager.

5 Interpersonal skills

The second aspect of personal power is the ability to inspire openness, empathy, firmness, flexibility, humour and (above all) interest in people.

5.1 Ability to inspire

If you can help your staff to become more involved and personally more responsible for the team's success, their performance will become better and better. You can do this by encouraging them to aspire to the three 'e's: **efficiency**, **effectiveness** and **excellence**. They must be able to:

■ look forward;
■ want to be the best;
■ know their job;
■ take responsibility for their part in moving the team forward.

You can learn more about how to inspire your team in the workbook *Motivating People* in this series.

5.2 Openness

You have seen earlier in this session that the only clue other people may have to how you are really feeling or thinking is your behaviour. If you are not open about your thoughts and feelings, then people will spend a lot of wasted time and effort trying to guess what you are up to. If you are open and up front about things, then others are likely to respond by being open too.

Gaining a reputation for being open and honest will result in people having much more confidence in your impartiality and fairness. They will then be more likely to look at things in an objective way and be prepared to negotiate constructively when the need arises.

5.3 Empathy

Activity 19   5 mins

Bridget Borland is a nurse at Westland General Hospital and has arrived at work feeling tired and upset. The reason is that she has spent most of last night at the hospital where her husband Liam was taken after a road accident. Having assured herself that his injuries aren't too serious (a broken leg and slight concussion) Bridget has decided to come into work to keep her mind off things.

Miranda is Bridget's ward manager. There have been several urgent new admissions, so she goes over to talk to Bridget as she takes off her coat. The conversation begins as follows.

Miranda: 'Good morning, Bridget. How are you today?'

Bridget: 'Well actually, Liam's been rushed into hospital and I've been up most of the night. . .'

Miranda: 'Sorry to hear that. Nothing too serious I hope. Listen, we've just had five urgent new admissions and I need you to get started straight away on initial checks for each patient. If you start now, you should be ready to prepare Mrs Jones for theatre by ten o'clock.'

Bridget: 'Well, I'm not sure. . .'

Miranda: 'I know you won't let me down. Tell me if there are any problems.'

Do you think Miranda did anything wrong? If you think so, how would you have handled things differently?

_____

_____

_____

How do you think Bridget will have reacted to this conversation?

_____

_____

_____

Managers are busy people and it's easy to get so concerned about the job that you forget that team members may have problems of their own.

Miranda showed no empathy – she didn't try to understand how Bridget was feeling. Bridget has had a shocking experience and may need someone to talk to. The lack of understanding by her ward manager is likely to make Bridget feel less inclined to put her best efforts into her work.

Managers who don't empathize with members of their team won't get the best from them. Miranda needs to develop the personal competency of relating to and showing sensitivity towards others.

5.4 Firmness

Firmness is an essential behaviour for every manager. You can only inspire confidence in your team if you are consistent in the decisions you make and constant in adhering to them.

To be firm in this way you need to be assertive, i.e. you need to believe that your needs and opinions are as important as those of other people. Conversely, if you think that your needs are less important, you are showing traits of submissiveness; if you think they are more important, you tend to be aggressive.

Activity 20 · 5 mins

Look at the following situations and decide what would be the assertive way to deal with them.

1 A new member of your team, Paul, is being confronted aggressively by Catherine, the leader of another team. The confrontation is loud, but Paul seems to be handling it. Do you:

a leave them alone; ☐

b interrupt and tell Catherine that she has no business talking to a member of your team like that; ☐

c sit them down and try to reason it out. ☐

2 You and your team have been working together for some time. In general everyone gets on very well, but two of the team tend to argue a lot. Do you:

a insist that they stop bickering and become friends; ☐

b leave it to them to sort it out; ☐

c sit them both down and talk it through. ☐

3 Arthur, a notoriously aggressive member of another department, is picking on Anne, a member of your team who is particularly timid. Anne isn't handling it very well, and you are getting very concerned. Do you:

a order Arthur to leave her alone; ☐

b ask Arthur to come and see you for a chat; ☐

c say nothing. ☐

In all three cases the best approach would be to get everyone involved to sit down and talk about the problem. If you ignore it you would be acting submissively and not giving your team members the support they deserve. On the other hand, if you take an aggressive stance you are simply encouraging the other parties to become even more entrenched in their positions without getting any nearer to a solution.

There are five golden rules for being assertive.

- Decide what you want to say, then say it specifically and directly.
- Stick to your argument, repeating it as often as is necessary.
- Assertively deflect any responses from the other person which might undermine your position.
- Use positive body language.
- Respect the rights of the other person.

Next time you are in a situation where you need to be assertive, follow these five golden rules. It may take some practice, but you will gain an increase in confidence and be able to set a standard of behaviour for others in your team to follow.

5.5 Flexibility

As individuals we often dislike change, but a good manager is always prepared for it.

Firmness and flexibility are two apparent opposites. How can a first line manager be both firm and flexible? Firmness has much to do with knowing what you want. Flexibility is needed in helping you get it.

You need to define your objectives in detail and then be firm about gearing all the actions of the team to meeting them. You need plans to achieve your objectives – but plans often go wrong. This is where the flexibility comes in: you have to be prepared to change your plans as necessary.

5.6 Humour

'If he makes me laugh, I'll probably vote for him. If he makes me think, I won't.'

First time voter at the 2001 general election.

Humour is often greatly underestimated as an interpersonal skill. However, it can be invaluable in creating a bond between you and your team members if it is used in the right way – and if you learn how to use it well.

Activity 21

3 mins

How do you think the use of humour can help you to be more effective as a first line manager?

_____

_____

_____

_____

Humour causes people to listen to you more closely. Humour helps people to learn. It also makes you seem more human, and can be used to make people feel that they are in a 'good' team. Also, people who are cheerful are more motivated and willing to do that bit extra for the team effort.

Some people are naturally funny. Others have to work at it.

Activity 22

3 mins

During the next few days, try out the following ideas.

- Notice how much you smile at people. Then try smiling some more.
- Be more relaxed with your team. Become more concerned, relaxed, open, friendly, interested and caring.
- Notice people whose attempts at humour make you wince. Think about why that is.
- Find out what makes you laugh. Do you have a dry wit or is your humour less subtle? Learn about your own sense of humour.
- Watch people who are naturally funny and have the same kind of humour as you. How do they make people laugh? Try out some of their techniques.
- Keep a note of funny things that happen during the day. This will help develop your sense of humour and provide you with anecdotes to use in future.
- Avoid telling jokes unless you are very good at it. Most people aren't.

5.7 Interest in people

Activity 23 · 3 mins

How much ought you to know about the individuals in your team? Place a 'Yes' in the appropriate boxes.

What I ought to know about the individuals in my team	As much as I can	As much as I can without prying	Little – it's none of my business
Their ambitions			
Their personal and domestic problems			
Their skills and experience			
Their interests and background			
The problems they may have in terms of equal work opportunities			
Any training they may be undertaking			
Their work problems			

Everything about a person can affect their work performance, so it is wrong to say that these matters are none of your business.

To get your team to respond in a positive way to your leadership, you have to show a genuine interest in them as people and build up a rapport with them.

You should try to know as much as possible about your team's:

> It could be argued that taking an interest in your team members is the most important part of your job as a manager.

- ambitions;
- skills and experience;
- training;
- work problems.

You can take an interest in the other areas so long as you don't pry. After all, everyone has a right to privacy.

Activity 24

10 mins

S/NVQ C9.1

This Activity may provide the basis of appropriate evidence for your S/NVQ portfolio. If you are intending to take this course of action, it might be better to write your answers on separate sheets of paper.

Go back to Activity 13 in which you identified the roles which the members of your team usually play.

Now do the same exercise again, but this time take the following into account.

1 Think about what roles each of them has the potential to play.

2 Decide what interpersonal skills they would need to develop to do so.

3 Decide what steps you could take to help them acquire those skills and behaviours. (Ideas to think about include arranging training courses, coaching and mentoring.)

Team member	Potential new role	Skills required	Steps to be taken to acquire them

6 Emotional intelligence

Emotional intelligence was first discussed in 1990 by researchers in the USA. It involves being aware of one's emotions and how they affect and interact with traditional intelligence (IQ). It has been found that people who are best at getting in touch with their own and other people's emotions are more successful both at work and in their social lives.

For example, research into the sales figures of a group of insurance salesmen showed that those who were 'in tune' with their emotions, who could manage their feelings well and who were optimistic sold 37% more insurance in their first two years than their less sensitive, pessimistic colleagues.

It is believed that emotional intelligence provides the bedrock for all the competencies we have looked at in this session. It is a new and important concept that will play an increasingly significant part in management theory in the years to come.

7 Developing a culture of trust

People will only work at their best when they feel safe.

If there is an atmosphere of trust and mutual respect in your team, everyone will be much more prepared to offer new ideas and try out new skills, knowing that, whatever happens, any response from the rest of the team will be positive and constructive.

But trust is an elusive thing. A great deal of effort is needed to establish it in the first place, and it can be destroyed in an instant.

You know enough about the skills of leadership by now to identify those factors that build trust in your team and those that can destroy it.

Activity 25

4 mins

Look at the words below, and write them in the appropriate boxes.

Factors that build trust	Factors that destroy trust

Rapport	Sarcasm	Respect	Eye contact	Uncertainty
Acceptance	One-way communication	Listening	Shared humour	Belonging
Criticism	Confidentiality	Innuendo	Consistency	Crossed wires
Constructive feedback	Accusation	Openness	Fault finding	Understanding

The answers can be found on page 117.

8 Confidentiality

Dictionary definitions of the word 'confidentiality' usually contain such words as 'classified', 'restricted', 'personal' and 'intimate'. These terms imply something that is secret or personal to the individual involved. But confidentiality also applies in the wider context to organizations and to the people in them.

As a first line manager you will learn many confidential details both about the work you are involved in and about members of your team.

8.1 Organizational confidentiality

Organizational confidentiality is usually governed by your contract of employment, and breach of corporate secrets will often result in dismissal for gross misconduct. In certain organizations, such as health and social services, it is part of the manager's job to share confidential information. For example, a care worker may have to share information about a client with other care workers and representatives from other agencies such as local authority housing departments. In these situations there will be a formal set of guidelines as to who can have access to the information.

8.2 Team confidentiality

You will sometimes receive personal information about your members of the workforce through counselling them during times of personal crisis and stress.

Whenever you become involved in counselling a member of your workforce, you must treat the information in complete confidence.

Activity 26

5 mins

Think about a recent situation when you have had to handle personal information relating to a member of your workforce. Answer the following questions about how you handled it.

Why was the information confidential?

_____

_____

How did you obtain the information?

_____

_____

Whom did you share it with?

_____

_____

Did you have the authority to share it?

_____

_____

It is sometimes difficult to decide whether a piece information you have received is confidential or not. In such situations there is a simple rule: never involve a third party without obtaining the permission of the person who gave you the information, or of the person who is the subject of the information.

8.3 Guidelines for handling confidential information

If in doubt about how to treat 'confidential' information in your possession, use the following checklist as a guide.

- Make sure you know what information is confidential and what is for general publication.
- If you are not certain whether a piece of organizational information is confidential, check with your manager – never assume that it is 'open'.
- If someone gives you information in confidence, never pass it to a third party without checking first with the person who confided in you.
- When you are away from your workplace, avoid discussing members of your workforce with your friends or colleagues.
- To foster a culture of trust and confidentiality within your workforce avoid discussing the personal affairs of individuals with anyone else who works with them.
- Never leave confidential notes or documents where others can see them.
- Make sure that any personal information relating to members of the workforce that is kept on a database is not accessible to non-authorized people.

8.4 Handling confessions

Occasionally members of your team may indicate that they want to confide in you something that could compromise you legally. For example, they might have stolen goods from the stock room or money from the till.

Telling you about it might make them feel better, but it puts you in the position of colluding in the wrongdoing.

Activity 27

3 mins

Lee is a credit controller in a large finance company. He has asked his first line manager, Sally, if he can have a quiet word with her. He tells her that he has done something terribly wrong and needs to tell someone about it. He says that she must promise not to tell anyone else about it. If you were Sally, how would you handle the situation?

By confessing to Sally, Lee is trying to make himself feel better by passing responsibility for the problem to Sally. But it would put Sally in an impossible situation, with her loyalty split between Lee and her employer. There is only one thing for her to do. Before he tells her anything, she must tell Lee that she cannot promise to keep his secret confidential. This then puts the ball back in his court, and it is up to him whether to 'come clean' with what he has done, or keep the information to himself.

Very often first line managers have access to information that is personal to members of their team but which is held on a corporate database. The type of information varies but, in certain circumstances, could relate to such matters as pay rates, employment history, disciplinary matters or even mortgage applications.

Activity 28

5 mins

Make a list of the types of confidential information you have on file about members of your team. Then make a note of how secure that information is from being accessed by unauthorized people.

9 Choosing your leadership style

It is no simple matter to define the term 'leader'. Perhaps the easiest approach is to see a leader more as a role with certain characteristic ways of behaving rather than as a particular type of person.

A good leader is one who adopts an appropriate style to suit the needs of the team and organization. And by 'style' we mean various bits and pieces of behaviour that, taken as a whole, create a clear, recognizable pattern.

Extensive research has found that there are a number of simple rules of behaviour, which together make up a successful leadership style. They are also a practical representation of all the ideas you have met so far in this session.

Activity 29  8 mins

Look at the rules of behaviour below, and tick the ones you think you follow already. Then divide the rest into groups of five and plan how you are going to introduce them, five at a time, into your everyday leadership style.

- Smile at people. ☐
- In a transaction, say the other person's name as soon as you can. ☐
- Avoid being judgemental about other people. ☐
- Acknowledge other people's ideas and build on them. ☐
- When you have made a mistake, admit it. ☐
- Use questions that are open-ended. ☐
- Look at the person you are talking to at least 60% of the time. ☐
- When you are listening, encourage the other person by saying 'Uh huh' or 'Really?'. ☐
- Lean towards the other person and keep your arms and legs uncrossed. ☐
- Be genuine. ☐
- Whenever appropriate, touch the other person. ☐

- Summarize what the other person has said to show that you have understood. ☐
- When talking to someone, refer back to what they have said previously. ☐
- Sit beside or at 90 degrees to the other person, not directly opposite them (which can feel confrontational). ☐
- If you disagree with someone, give the reason **before** saying that you disagree. ☐
- Whenever possible give the other person something, even if it is just a few notes. ☐
- Show rapport by saying that you understand how the other person is feeling and why. ☐

So, as a first line manager, if you want to adopt a style which will help you to generate appropriate behaviour in your workforce (or anybody else) just follow the rules above. (Some of them relate to the use of body language, which we will cover in more detail in Session C.)

Self-assessment 2

12 mins

1 Behaviour breeds _____

2 What **five** roles are normally found in a strong team?

_____

_____

3 First line managers who want _____ from their team must be _____ in return.

4 First line managers who show _____ get respect.

5 A first line manager needs to be _____ in putting the achievement of the team's objectives above everything else.

6 Taking an _____ in members of the workforce is arguably the most important job a first line manager in his/her role as _____ has to do.

7 Which **seven** of the following interpersonal skills are the most important for a first line manager to have?

Flexibility ☐
Ability to inspire ☐
Brusqueness ☐
Skill at winning arguments ☐
Openness ☐
Public speaking ☐
Interest in people ☐
Immovability ☐
Empathy ☐
Good body language ☐
Friendliness ☐
Firmness ☐
Humour ☐

Answers to these questions can be found on page 115.

10 Summary

- There are three kinds of need for human contact.

  - Joining and belonging – the need for group contact.
  - Role and control – the need to have a clear role or control of others.
  - Pairing and sharing – the need for individual contacts on a one-to-one basis.

- As a first line manager, you can improve your leadership skills by developing:

  - personal qualities of loyalty, dependability, integrity, fairness and determination;
  - skills at dealing with people that include ability to inspire, openness, empathy, firmness, flexibility, humour and an interest in people.

- According to research into the concept of emotional intelligence, people who are best at getting in touch with their own and other people's emotions are more successful both at work and in their social lives.

- You should never pass confidential information to a third party without obtaining the permission of the person who gave you the information, or the person who is the subject of the information.

- A 'leader' can be seen as a role with certain characteristic ways of behaving rather than as a particular type of person.

Session C
How to get the result you want

1 Introduction

As a first line manager you have a number of means at your disposal to get people to do what you want. Sometimes they will respond just as you intended, sometimes not. Sometimes it will involve a lot of effort on your part, sometimes you may even have to compromise. Your success will largely depend on the skills you will learn in this session.

We will consider four ways of getting other people to do what you want.

- Instructing – where you have sufficient power and authority to **tell** someone what to do.
- Influencing – where you bring the whole context of the situation to bear on the other person, including the quality of your past and current working relationship, his or her wants, needs and fears.
- Persuading – where you use your all your verbal and non-verbal skills to get the other person to agree.
- Negotiating – where you have the same bargaining power as the other person, and both of you have to compromise in order to get something of what each of you wants.

2 Instructing

As a first line manager you have the power to issue instructions to your workforce. There are a number of ways of getting the message across, some of them more effective than others. Three of these ways are:

- giving orders;
- making a request;
- pleading.

2.1 Orders

We give an order when:

- it's an emergency – where timing is critical;
- an immediate response is needed;
- the people on the receiving end know exactly how to respond.

An example of an order might be:

'Take aim. Fire!'

Orders are right for such jobs as the armed services, police or fire services because there's no time for requests or explanations – an immediate response is needed. Because of the urgency, an order has to be short and to the point. It must also be precise. The normal courtesies of 'please' and 'thank you' are neglected and yet, in circumstances where giving an order is warranted, this is quite acceptable. It is also acceptable in a situation where one person has specialist knowledge and is training someone else how to do something (for example, 'Now, double-click the mouse on the file name, then . . .').

Most of the time, however, orders aren't a suitable way of getting things done. In most circumstances, people will respond more positively if they are involved in the decision-making and understand the reason why something needs to be done.

2.2 Requests

Usually people will respond better if they are **asked** to do something rather than if they are **told** to do it.

This doesn't undermine your power as a manager. A request can easily make clear what you want done, when, why, how and by whom. Giving your instructions in the form of requests doesn't mean that you lose any of your control over the job.

Asking rather than telling makes the team feel that you see them as people with something to offer to the job rather than just cogs in a wheel.

Activity 30

3 mins

Here are two very different ways of giving the same instruction. Which do you think is better, and why?

a 'Fred, you're on the gate from 10.30. Hand over to Mr Khan at mid-day.'

b 'I'd like you to go on the gate this morning, Fred. Do 10.30 to mid-day and then hand over to Mr Khan, would you? . . . Thanks.'

The obvious difference between the two versions is that the first one is an order, the second is a request because it features:

- a question rather than a statement;
- a more personal kind of language ('I'd like you to . . .');
- a politer turn of phrase;
- a pause, during which the speaker checks Fred's understanding and agreement.

That's all a request need be – a matter of saying 'I'd like you to. . .' or 'Would you. . .', or 'Would you mind. . .' rather than just 'Do this'. But it lets people know that you value them as well as the job. And saying 'Thank you' reminds everyone that you are all human beings who respond best when treated with courtesy.

2.3 Pleading

Sometimes, when you are tired or under pressure, you may feel that the best way to get something done is to plead with the person concerned.

Activity 31

A team leader makes the following plea to the computer operator.

'Look, I know that you've been busy, but this job is really urgent. Customer services will be furious if the figures aren't ready by tomorrow morning. So, for my sake, please try and speed it up.'

What do you think about this as a way of getting people to do something for you? What effect would it have on the relationship between you and them?

Well, we have all probably tried to give an instruction in this kind of way at some point, and it may even have worked. But it's a bad idea to try to lead people on the basis of their sympathy or liking for you because:

- by pleading you run the risk that it may reduce your personal power;
- it may appear that you are handing over both control and authority to that person;
- asking someone to carry out a task as a personal favour could place professional working relationships at risk;
- if you ask for favours, sooner or later you will be obliged to return them.

56

You may be able to use the power of your position to get someone to do something, but it doesn't help you to control **how** they do it. And if you had no power over them, they may not do it at all. In these situations you need to use your personal power to come to an agreement with them. To do this you need to acquire the skills of influencing and persuading.

3 Influencing

By 'influencing' we mean trying to affect someone's behaviour by changing their thoughts, beliefs or attitudes.

Activity 32

3 mins

Write down four factors that made you apply for, and then accept, your current job.

_____

_____

_____

_____

You might have mentioned the reputation of the organization, type of work, location of the job, salary, career prospects, opportunities to learn a new skill, and so on. They could all be factors that play a part in influencing your decision to take the job.

You can use influencing factors to great effect in the workplace when you are negotiating with other people. (You will learn more about the specific techniques involved in the negotiating process on page 71.)

By learning about influencing factors you can:

- create a situation in which your skills of persuasion and negotiation will be most effective;
- recognize the factors that might influence **you** in a negotiating situation.

The main factors that influence us are as follows:

- personal relationships;
- position power;
- formality;
- knowledge and expertise;
- gender, race and age;
- reputation;
- expectations about outcomes;
- pressure of work and deadlines;
- location.

We will look at each of these in turn.

3.1 Personal relationships

EXTENSION 3
You can learn more about influencing factors in *Negotiating Persuading and Influencing* by Alan Fowler.

Your relationship with the person you are dealing with can have a significant influence on your communication tactics. It can work in the following two ways.

- If relations have been friendly in the past, both of you will begin with the assumption that this will continue, and will make an effort for it do so. If relations have been antagonistic, you will be half expecting the same again, and your words and body language are likely to reflect this.
- If you anticipate that this will be one of a long series of dealings in the future, you will be at pains to keep the relationship friendly, whatever your inner feelings may be.

Personal relationships are particularly important in a close-knit environment such as a team. Whether people like or dislike each other can have a major influence on the team's cohesion, and it can be difficult to work objectively with someone with whom you have a personal problem.

3.2 Position power

Everyone in an organization has the power to influence others. The higher up the organization they are, the more power and influence they have. This, as you saw in Session A, is known as 'position power'.

However, while some people enjoy influence because of their position in the management hierarchy, others have it because they have a particular type of job in the organization.

Activity 33

3 mins

Who else at work has influence over you besides the people who are in a higher managerial position than you?

_____

_____

_____

Your suggestions might include the following.

- Security staff: if a security guard insists on searching your bag as you enter the building, you probably won't argue about it.
- The human resource department: if the HR officer tells you that recruitment must be done in a certain way according to company policy, you would probably accept this.
- Experts in IT and other specialists.

If you look at your list, you will see that there two groups.

- People who hold a special position (such as security staff and inspectors).
- People who have special expertise (such as IT experts).

Both groups have the power through their position or expertise to influence the minds and actions of others in the organization.

As far as dealing with other managers in the hierarchy is concerned, there are several strategies at your disposal. Some will be particularly effective when your position power is high. Others will depend more on using personal power.

The strategies include:

- assertiveness – most frequently used when position power is high but success will be difficult to achieve;
- friendliness – often used when both position power and expectations of success are low;
- reason – used frequently when position power and expectations of success are high;
- bargaining;
- referral to a higher authority;
- sanctions or disciplinary action.

One more important point – organizational 'politics' can come into play when you are dealing with a relatively junior colleague who has close connections with senior management. Although this should make no difference to the way you behave, you may well feel that you must be careful of what you say or do.

3.3 Formality

Some people can be overawed if they have to take part in formal communications (such as trades union negotiations). The process is usually more structured than in informal situations, and more people may be involved, but the basic skills are just the same as when you are dealing with a colleague in the workplace. So don't let formal conditions influence your approach.

3.4 Knowledge and expertise

Any expert knowledge you have in the subject under discussion will give you a greater sense of confidence, and this will show in your body language and tone of voice. Expert knowledge is particularly valuable if you are suffering under the negative influences of weak position power or poor personal relationships.

Activity 34

5 mins

Think of a recent situation where you have had to take part in discussions on a topic in which you are a real expert. Then compare it with a time when you had to do the same involving a topic you knew little about. How did you feel in each situation? Could you have prepared yourself better for the second situation? If so, how?

Situation 1

_____

_____

_____

Situation 2

_____

_____

_____

You would probably have done better in the second situation if you had done some research first, and you would certainly have found the experience more satisfying.

3.5 Gender, race and age

The influence of gender, race and age on negotiations can be subtle, but is very common, none the less. It can affect both sides, causing one person to feel dominant and the other to feel threatened, with the result that the former may become more aggressive and the latter submissive.

Such discrimination can be difficult to counter as it is often not overtly stated, but shows itself more in a general attitude of superiority. If you come across this type of influence, either in yourself or others, you need to recognize it for what it is and make a conscious effort to eliminate it from your working environment. You can learn more about handling discrimination in _Commitment to Equality_ in this series.

3.6 Reputation

If the most important thing to you is to gain a reputation as a hard bargainer, or as someone who always gets what they want, you may be storing up trouble for the future. You can't always win, and if you are known as someone who takes a hard line, others will be far less willing to compromise, and conflicts are more likely to arise. Much better to aim for a reputation for fair dealing and problem-solving.

3.7 Expectations about outcomes

Don't be too fixed about your desired outcome. If you have decided beforehand what this is going to be, you will be less inclined to be flexible when alternative solutions appear. And, however confident you are of the strength of your argument, there is always a danger that some factor will emerge which you have not anticipated.

When it comes to formal negotiations, it is always good to know what your limits are, and to be flexible within them. You will learn more about this later on in this session.

3.8 Pressure of work and deadlines

Making decisions under pressure of a deadline can have advantages and disadvantages.

Activity 35

3 mins

Can you think of one advantage of a tight deadline in decision-making and one disadvantage?

Advantage

Disadvantage

One advantage could be that, if you have prepared your case thoroughly, you may be able to push a decision through before the other side has had time to think out all the implications.

A disadvantage could be that decisions made under pressure may not satisfy either party in the long run. It is unlikely that all the factors will have been fully explored, so the optimum solution for both parties will not have been identified, and the other party may be left resentful and ready for revenge at a later date.

3.9 Location

The influence of location can be very strong for some people – whether it is the general layout of the office environment or, more specifically, the location in which discussions take place.

Some people may feel more confident on their home territory. They also have the advantage of immediate access to files, plans and other information which might be useful. On the other hand, they might gather a great deal of background information by going to the other party's offices, and be more able to control the point in the discussions at which the meeting comes to an end.

The layout of the meeting area also can also be a strong influence on what happens during a discussion session.

Activity 36

2 mins

Assuming that there are just two people involved, which of the following seating arrangements would provide the most constructive environment to carry out discussions? Put a circle round the one you think is best.

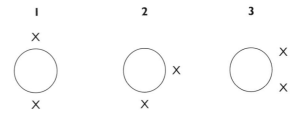

63

You should have chosen the second option. This gives the parties the best chance of building a rapport. Option 1, where they sit opposite each other, tends to give a feeling of confrontation – as though battle lines have been drawn. In option 3 they are sitting next to each other. This may avoid the confrontation problem but their close proximity may be constricting and they will be unable to use body language, such as eye contact, to check each other's reactions and understanding.

3.10 Using influence to promote action

Activity 37

3 mins

In each of the following situations, identify the factors used to influence team members to carry out the decision in the way the manager wants. Use the list of influencing factors discussed in this session,

a Frances Dean commands the respect of her team members. They are convinced about her ability, and aim to be loyal. She uses this influence to encourage her staff to implement decisions.

_____

_____

b Marco Luciana recognizes that his team would be more able to implement decisions if he re-organized the office layout. This will bring certain team members closer together and improve communication between them.

_____

_____

c Daniel Patterson is very highly trained in logistics and this expertise is recognized by his team. As a result, team members listen carefully to his suggestions and explanations on how to carry out certain operations.

_____

_____

You should have recognized that:

- method (a) involves the influence of personal relationships;
- method (b) involves the influence of location;
- method (c) involves the influence of expertise.

4 Persuading

Personal power is vital in all communication, whether it is formal or informal, to one person or to a thousand. Even if you have the best idea, the best strategy or the best product, you will get a much better result if you are able to get other people to 'buy in' to the idea. And getting people to buy in involves the skill of persuasion.

If you are going to persuade someone to do something you must first decide the following.

1 What objective you want to achieve.

2 What behaviour you want from the other person which will allow you to achieve your objective.

Once you are clear about these two things, you can concentrate on choosing the techniques that will persuade the other person to help you achieve your objective.

Persuasion techniques can be verbal or non-verbal.

4.1 Verbal persuasion techniques

The high street bookshops are full of books containing hints and tips on how to get ahead in business. Many of them describe weird and wonderful techniques that may work for the author, but would be totally inappropriate in your own work place. One thing that they nearly all emphasize, however, is the importance of good verbal communication in getting what you want.

Verbal communication techniques fall into three groups:

- building rapport;
- boosting the other party's self-esteem;
- creating a positive atmosphere.

Building rapport

If you have a rapport with someone it means that you are on the same wave length as they are.

When building rapport, first impressions are all important. When you meet someone for the first time you pick up and give out all sorts of messages about each other without really noticing it. What you look like, the sound of your voice, mannerisms, and so on. This information is then processed internally and conclusions drawn as to whether you like or dislike the other person – and consequently whether you are going to get on with them or not.

Activity 38

5 mins

Imagine that a new recruit is due to join your team tomorrow morning. What verbal behaviour could you adopt to make her feel at ease – to build a rapport – as soon as she arrives? Try to think of four suggestions.

_____

_____

_____

_____

Your suggestions could have included:

- expressing pleasure at her arrival;
- chatting about everyday things that you both have in common (such as travelling to work);
- using her name frequently (when talking both to her and to other members of the team);
- asking a small favour of her – this will help her to feel valued;
- using appropriate humour to relax the situation;
- showing empathy, i.e. showing that you can understand how she is feeling.

You can also use a number of non-verbal techniques. These are discussed later on in this section.

Boosting the other party's self esteem

EXTENSION 4
You may like to read
How to be Twice as Smart
by Scott Witt. It is one
of many books which
give helpful ideas on
getting ahead in the
work place.

According to Scott Witt, one of the most effective ways of influencing people is to make them feel good about themselves. For example, you can simply ask someone to do something for you in such a way that they become anxious to do it because it makes them feel important.

You can boost someone's self-esteem by, for example:

- making them believe that they have a reputation to live up to;
- making them feel needed;
- asking questions that make them feel knowledgeable;
- making them feel that there is a challenge to be met.

Activity 39

3 mins

Next time you ask members of your workforce to do something, try saying something to boost their self-esteem first. Notice how much more enthusiastic they are about doing what you ask.

Creating a positive atmosphere

If you follow a few simple rules, you will find it is easy to create a positive atmosphere that encourages co-operation.

1   Use phrases such as 'We could. . .' or 'How would you feel if . . .' rather than 'You must. . .' or 'I can't. . .'. This will instil a feeling of collaboration rather than opposition in negotiations.

2   Make it clear that you are prepared to consider the other party's arguments constructively, and acknowledge that they have a valid viewpoint.

3   Give the other side the chance to talk without interrupting. You will learn much and avoid creating an atmosphere of dissent.

Neuro-linguistic programming

Neuro-linguistic programming (NLP) is a rather forbidding name for something quite straightforward. It is the term used for a study of the relationship between thinking, language and behaviour – **what** people do, **why** they do it and **how** they do it.

EXTENSION 5
A useful introduction to neuro-linguistic programming is given in *Introducing NLP* by Sue Knight.

Put very simply, by studying how people behave, you can tell what they are thinking. And, conversely, by behaving in a particular way you can influence how other people think. We have already seen how you can build rapport with another person by using eye contact, finding common topics of conversation and making them feel needed. In fact, most of us do this all the time without even realizing it. NLP takes the idea much further and can be an invaluable tool in developing relationships with other people in the organization. NLP is dealt with in more detail in *Networking and Sharing Information* in this series.

4.2 Non-verbal persuasion techniques

The final skill you need in order to master the art of persuasion is the use of non-verbal communication.

Research shows that less than half of communication is through what you have to say. The rest is partly communicated through the way you look and partly through the way you act, and more tends to be conveyed by appearance than by action.

Clearly, then, appearance is a vital element in persuading people to behave in the way you want.

The diagram below shows how your appearance affects the way you see yourself, and how this, in turn, affects how others see you. If you look and act

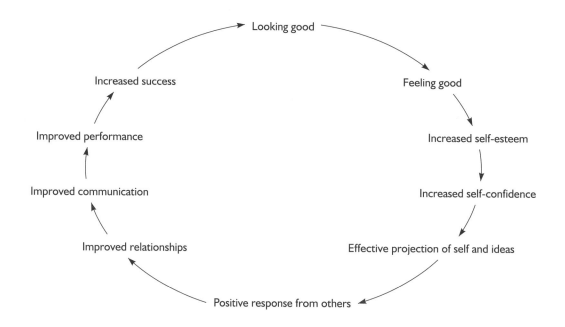

as though you are successful you will feel successful, if you feel successful then people will assume that you are successful, and so on.

You can communicate non-verbal messages about yourself in many ways. Some of the most important include using your:

- eyes;
- facial expression;
- voice;
- gestures;
- posture;
- appearance.

Eyes

EXTENSION 6
How to Communicate Effectively by Bert Decker is a highly readable guide to the use of body language and non-verbal communication.

In general, your eyes are the only part of you that directly connect with the person you are talking to. You can use your eyes to intimidate, build rapport, plead, show affection or fear. It largely depends on the length of time you maintain eye contact.

In one-to-one conversations, you should make eye contact for between five and ten seconds at a time. You may want to practise this with a friend, to get a sense of what it feels like.

Facial expression

You may think that you are a natural 'smiler', but research has shown that only about a third of people naturally smile most of the time, while a third are neutral and a third smile very little.

An open, smiling expression makes you appear friendly and, as the Book of Proverbs says: 'He who would have friends, let him show himself friendly'. It has also been claimed that smiling actually makes you feel more cheerful and positive.

You may find it helpful to ask other people which third of the 'smilers' you belong to. Then, if necessary, practise smiling more – even when you don't feel like it. You will find that it makes you feel better.

Voice

Your voice is a tool, which you can use to great effect if you know how. It conveys energy, emotion and mood. Research shows that, in situations where the other person can't see you (such as during a telephone conversation), your tone and intonation convey 84% of the message they receive.

Activity 40 · 5 mins

Next time you ring someone up and they respond by saying 'Hello', think about what clues their voice is giving out about their feelings, mood, confidence and attitude towards you. Then try to be aware of the messages you are sending through your own voice.

Gestures

Your gestures should reflect the energy you feel inside. Italians use their hands, arms and facial expressions to support what they are saying, and this not only reinforces their verbal message, but it keeps the listener's attention and introduces an emotional factor which makes what they say far more arresting. Arms flung wide and eyes cast to heaven cannot fail to attract the listener's attention.

On the other hand, physical habits such as rocking from one foot to the other, rattling money in your pockets or scratching your head can be very distracting and should be avoided.

Activity 41 · 3 mins

Ask your friends to tell you if you have any physical mannerism that you are not aware of. Then try to notice every time you do it so that, gradually, you can stop doing it altogether.

Posture

Everyone has their own style of posture and movement, but some give out messages that you would rather not send. Standing in a slumped position is very negative and often implies low self-esteem. It also suggests that you are uninterested and lacking in energy – not a good idea if you want to give an air of self-confidence. Let's face it, you never see a politician or celebrity slumping!

The best position is to stand upright with your weight slightly forward and balanced equally on both feet. Avoid crossing your arms or legs, as these can appear as a defensive barrier against other people.

Appearance

Whatever the way you dress, it should be appropriate for the environment in which you work. Your appearance says a lot about how you feel about yourself.

It reflects your general attitude so, if you dress sloppily, others will perceive you as a sloppy manager. If you dress smartly the impression you give will be far more dynamic and positive. The same principle applies whether the organization dress code is formal or casual.

Think about your normal appearance at work. What impression do you give? Are you always well groomed, with well-pressed clothes and well-cut hair? Do you dress in that particular style because you always have done, or because you know it suits you? Are the colours you wear the right ones for you? Are some of your clothes really past their wear-by date?

You could ask other people to honestly give an opinion about your appearance. Consider having a colour analysis session. It can be very helpful in identifying colours and styles that really do you justice.

5 Negotiating

King Solomon was faced with a problem. Two women had come to him seeking justice, both claiming that they were the mother of the same baby boy. How did Solomon solve the problem? Well, he pronounced that the only fair thing to do was to divide the baby in half and give one half to each woman. Faced with the prospect of the death of her child, the real mother renounced her rights. Solomon deduced from this that she was the true mother.

King Solomon was a past master at resolving conflict through negotiation. He listened to both arguments, identified the facts, and found a solution that was fair to both sides.

This section looks at negotiation – the skill of finding a solution to conflicting needs and wants which, while not always giving either party everything they want, at least usually provides them with enough to feel that they have received what is fair.

Negotiating is only necessary when you don't have enough positional power to get what you want by simply issuing an instruction.

5.1 The nature of negotiation

Louise asks one of her team, Nico, to take part in a market research project that will involve him in about 10 hours' work a week for seven weeks. Nico is interested, but points out that being on the project will mean 10 hours a week less in which to do his normal job.

Louise expects this. Her response is to offer Nico some extra clerical help, but Nico feels that this will still leave him about five hours a week short.

Louise suggests that Nico can probably cope with this. Nico is reluctant.

Louise points out that being on the market research project will be useful career move for Nico. Nico agrees and thanks Louise for the opportunity but says that he is still concerned about the additional pressure and the possibility of his normal work falling behind.

The two colleagues consider several options.

Louise finally bridges the gap by agreeing to transfer one of Nico's routine tasks to another colleague, Grace, for the duration of the project, on condition that Nico spends a reasonable amount of time training and briefing Grace in how to do it.

This kind of 'dealing', which goes on a lot at work, is a classic example of negotiation.

All negotiations have five main characteristics.

- There is a gap to be bridged between two (and sometimes more) positions.
- Both sides recognize that it is desirable to reach an agreement.
- Both sides are willing to make concessions in order to reach agreement.
- Neither side knows in advance how much the other is willing to concede.
- The negotiation process consists of repeated exchanges of messages.

Both sides in a negotiation should set themselves SMART objectives.

Specific
Measurable
Achievable
Relevant
Time bound

The outcome of negotiations should be a decision which is, in the circumstances, satisfactory to both sides.

Usually this means a compromise of some kind. Typically, each side enters the negotiations recognizing that they may not get everything they want. On the other hand, each will have a limit beyond which they are not willing to go.

Negotiations may be formal or informal.

5.2 Formal negotiation

Some of the negotiations you may become involved in at work may be formal, for example when:

- discussing changes to pay and conditions with union or staff association representatives;
- seeking an agreement with suppliers or customers over contract terms or compensation for poor work;
- agreeing the terms for a collaborative venture.

Often such negotiations will be carried out in accordance with formal guidelines and with specified personnel involved. They may even involve an external body which is highly skilled in such negotiations, such as the Advisory, Conciliation and Arbitration Service (ACAS) or a trade union.

Activity 42 · 5 mins

Make a note of any formal negotiations that you or your colleagues have recently been involved in at work. Who took part? Were they conducted according to formal guidelines? Was any external body involved? Did each side feel satisfied with the outcome?

_____

_____

_____

_____

_____

5.3 Informal negotiation

Most of the time the negotiations you become involved in will be informal rather than formal.

A great deal of your time as a first line manager will be taken up in negotiating with your team in regard to such matters as:

- work load;
- time off;
- working conditions;
- co-operative projects.

Whether the negotiations are formal or informal, the same basic process applies.

5.4 Six stages of negotiation

The size and complexity of negotiations can vary enormously: from international conferences of global significance at one extreme to planning a staff outing at the other. But whatever their size, all negotiations will go through the same six stages.

- Preparation.
- Exchanging initial views.
- Exploring possible solutions.
- Identifying common ground.
- Reaching a compromise.
- Implementing the compromise.

While we look briefly at each one in turn, check back to the case study of Louise and Nico to see how it works in practice.

Step		Action
1	Prepare	■ Know your stuff. Don't get caught out by unexpected revelations from the other side. ■ Decide your objectives – what is the least you will settle for? ■ What will your strategy be?
2	Exchange initial views	■ Give a brief statement of your starting position. ■ Find out about the other side by getting them to talk about their concerns, motives and aims. Try to identify their strengths and weaknesses. ■ Clarify the size of the gap between you.
3	Explore possible solutions	■ Consider all possible compromises without committing either side. ■ Point out the benefits of finding a mutually satisfactory solution. ■ Encourage the other person to make constructive suggestions. ■ Find out what the other side values that it costs you little to give.
4	Identify common ground	■ Find out what you both agree on and then build on it.
5	Reach a compromise	■ Use your skills of persuasion to encourage the other side to reach a compromise. ■ If necessary, give a small concession to avoid them losing face.
6	Implement the compromise	■ Write down and confirm the details of what has been agreed. ■ Agree a timetable for implementation. ■ If the compromise is complicated, agree a detailed plan which includes: actions to be taken, deadlines, who will be involved, who will be informed, how the plan will be monitored and evaluated.

5.5 Negotiating skills

In Session B you learned about certain behaviours which would build an atmosphere of trust and co-operation in your team, but there are other behaviours that are particularly useful in negotiating. They are as follows.

Concentrate on the reasons behind the other side's stance rather than the stance itself

If, say, a team member asks for more pay, look at the whole picture rather than just the pay demand itself. For instance, if you discover that the additional money is needed because of child care problems, it may be that other factors can be brought into the negotiations in order to find a solution, such as holiday allowances or flexitime.

Attack the problem rather than the person

Don't get involved in a spiral of personal attacks. That does no good to anyone, and takes the focus away from the problem itself.

Move the discussion forward rather than getting trapped in counter-arguments

There is no benefit in simply disagreeing with the other side's position. You should aim to look for ways of finding an area of common ground, then move forward from there.

State your reasons first, then disagree

The phrase 'No, I disagree' is like a brick wall. It brings the other party to a full stop without offering any way forward. Much better to give your reasons for disagreeing first, then say that you disagree. You could say, for example, 'While you say that the yarn is stripey because of our poor spinning, it could be that your tufting machine is not working properly. So I can't agree. . .'.

Never exaggerate

We have already learned that behaviour breeds behaviour. So, if you exaggerate the facts, the other side will too. Once you have lost sight of the real facts, you cannot negotiate a lasting solution.

Remember the value of openness

In Session B we learned that if you are open in the way you communicate, the other side is much more likely to be objective in the negotiations.

Use questions as a negotiating tool

Never assume that you know all there is to know about the other side's position. Ask questions to discover their motives, beliefs, prejudices, and bargaining strengths and weaknesses. By asking questions you move the focus away from your own position, and may discover new areas of agreement which could move the negotiations forward.

Keep checking

Make sure that you summarize the position at regular intervals so that both sides know exactly where they are. Any progress you make thereafter will be based on a solid foundation.

It is important to remember that successful negotiations depend on both sides paying very careful attention to what the other side is saying. In order to get a precise understanding, they need to ask each other many kinds of question, such as those that follow.

- Reflecting   'So what you're saying is. . .'
- Supporting   'Yes, that's a very positive suggestion. So can we. . .?'
- Disagreeing   'Won't that cost too much?'
- Constructing   'Would it help if. . .?'
- Clarifying   'Isn't the point that. . .?'
- Interpreting   'Are you suggesting. . ..?'
- Confirming   'So we agree that. . .'
- Testing   'Would it be right to say that. . .?'

Activity 43  5 mins

Make a note of the eight behaviours listed above. Next time you are involved in negotiations with someone, either at work or at home, use the list as a memory jogger of the behaviours you should be adopting. Then make a brief note of those which worked well and those in which you need more practice.

Randolph Provisions are negotiating the price on the purchase of corned beef from a new supplier. Their buyer is prepared to pay a maximum of £0.39 per tin for 22,000 packs of 24 tins, but her objective is to get the price down to £0.35. The supplier's salesman is prepared to accept a minimum of £0.37, but is aiming to achieve £0.41. However, he will accept a slightly lower price if the order quantity is higher.

Activity 44  3 mins

The two negotiators can reach agreement across a range of prices.

What is the maximum price in this range?

What is the minimum price in this range?

The range within which the agreed price will fall is the area where the buyer's and the supplier's maximum and minimum prices overlap. We can show this negotiable area in a table below, with a dash indicating a price that one or other side is not prepared to consider.

Buyer's range	35	36	37	38	39	–	–
Supplier's range	–	–	37	38	39	40	41

The price range is therefore between 37 pence and 39 pence, but remember that neither side actually knows where the other's maximum and minimum lie.

It is up to the two negotiators to use their skills to try to persuade each other in the direction of the most favourable outcome for themselves. Above 39 pence and below 37 pence, agreement is, of course, not possible.

Activity 45

3 mins

What would happen if there were a stalemate, for example if the buyer refused to go above £0.36?

_____

_____

_____

The supplier might agree to shift his minimum price downwards if:

- the buyer increased the order quantity;
- the buyer agreed to a long-term contract;
- the buyer agreed to take some other product from the supplier as well.

Activity 46

30 mins

S/NVQ C1.1

This Activity will help you to review what you have learned so far about personal qualities. It could provide the basis of appropriate evidence for your S/NVQ portfolio. If you are intending to take this course of action, it might be better to write your answers on separate sheets of paper.

1   Think about an improvement that would really help your team to carry out their tasks better. It might be new equipment, different working conditions or some other change in the current system.

2   Decide who the gate-keepers are, i.e. who has the power to grant you permission to make the improvement.

3   Carry out the necessary negotiations with the gatekeepers, keeping a record of what happens during each of the six stages of negotiation.

Self-assessment 3

12 mins

1 State whether each of the following is a command, a request or a plea.

a 'Prepare this order for Mentrim Ltd, would you?' _____

b 'Don't argue, just do it!' _____

c 'Please do your best to get this done on time. It's for the good of the whole team, you know!' _____

d 'Can you just adjust this so that the legs don't protrude? Thanks.' _____

2 Which one of the following is the best advice to a first line manager when team members haven't carried out a task they have been asked to do?

a Ask someone else to do the job.

b Ask the team members whether your instructions were clear.

c Initiate immediate disciplinary action.

d Reconsider your decision and look at alternatives.

3 Suggest two situations when expert knowledge might be particularly valuable.

a _____

b _____

4 Suggest three ways in which you can boost someone's self-esteem.

a _____

b _____

c _____

5 You can use neuro-linguistic programming to build a _____ with someone.

6 Suggest six ways in which you can use non-verbal communication to influence someone's behaviour towards you.

7 If one side clearly loses in negotiations, what two risks are being run?

   a _____

   b _____

8 What are the six steps in negotiation?

   1 _____

   2 _____

   3 _____

   4 _____

   5 _____

   6 _____

Answers to these questions can be found on pages 115–116.

6 Summary

- There are four ways of achieving what you want at work.

  - Instructing – where you have sufficient power and authority to **tell** someone what to do.
  - Influencing – where you bring the whole context of the situation to bear on the other person, including the quality of your past and current working relationship, his or her wants, needs and fears.
  - Persuading – where you use your all your verbal and non-verbal skills to get the other person to agree.
  - Negotiating – where you each have the same bargaining power, and each has to compromise in order to get something of what you want.

- Requests are generally the most suitable way of making your requirements known. They should:

  - be polite and personal;
  - leave time for questions and a reply.

- The main factors of influence are:

  - personal relationships;
  - position power;
  - formality;
  - knowledge and expertise;
  - gender, race and age;
  - reputation;
  - expectations about outcomes;
  - pressure of work and deadlines;
  - location.

- If you are going to persuade someone you must first decide:

  - what objective you want to achieve;
  - what behaviour you want from that other person which will allow you to achieve your objective.

- Verbal influencing techniques include:

  - building rapport;
  - boosting the other party's self-esteem;
  - creating a constructive environment.

- Neuro-linguistic programming (NLP) is a study of the relationship between thinking, language and behaviour – **what** people do, **why** they do it and **how** they do it.

- Non-verbal influencing techniques include communicating with your:

  - eyes;
  - facial expression;
  - voice;
  - gestures;
  - posture;
  - appearance.

■ Negotiations are a specialized kind of meeting. They depend heavily on clear communication and accurate understanding. Negotiators typically question each other closely, and repeat and summarize ideas in order to ensure that they have not misunderstood one another.

■ The agreements reached during negotiations need to be recorded with care.

■ The six stages of negotiation are:

- preparation;
- exchange of initial views;
- exploring possible solutions;
- identifying common ground;
- reaching a compromise;
- implementing the compromise.

Session D
Managing conflict

1 Introduction

In primitive times man dealt with conflict in one of two ways – fight or flight. It worked quite well at the time, the strongest won and everyone knew where they were. But society today is far more complex than before, and different solutions are needed. Fight and flight (at least within most societies) have been replaced by negotiation – which you learned about in Session C.

But what happens when negotiation fails?

This final session brings together all the skills you have learned so far and applies them to the management of conflict in the workplace. You will learn what causes conflict, what steps can be taken to handle it, and how you can make sure that everyone ends up with at least something of what they want.

2 The value of personal power

In earlier sessions of this workbook you learned about the different types of power which can enable you as a first line manager to manage your workforce. They included:

- position power – the power that comes with the job;
- expert power – acquired through being an expert in your job;
- personal power – acquired through development of personal qualities and interpersonal skills.

You may well hold all three types of power. You certainly hold position power by the very nature of your managerial role.

Activity 47 · ⏱ 3 mins

Read the comments of the two first line managers below, then decide what type/s of power they each hold.

Simon, assistant manager in a small supermarket:

'I always try to consult my staff, but in the end they do what I say because I am the boss.'

James: first line manager in a tufting department of a carpet manufacturer:

'I'm not always sure what I should do in certain work situations. Even when I am reasonably sure, it's not always easy to get my team to do what I want.'

We can assume that both James and Simon hold **expert power** since they would not be first line managers if they were not experts in their fields. They should also both have **position power** simply by the fact that they are managers.

Simon consults his team when he thinks it appropriate, and has enough **personal power** to be assertive when the need arises. He seems to have the balance about right.

On the other hand it looks as though James is unable to use either his position power to enforce his decisions or his personal power to get his team to buy in to them. His lack of effective influencing, persuading and negotiating skills means that he will not find it at all easy to solve any dispute that arises with his team.

So it is clear that, while it's useful to have expert power and position power as a first line manager, to be able to negotiate a resolution to a conflict situation you also need personal power.

3 Causes of conflict

Sometimes the odds on negotiations being successful are reduced, not because of the lack of skill on behalf of the negotiators, but for reasons which may be beyond their control. The main causes are as follows:

- opposing objectives;
- values being threatened;
- feedback being taken as criticism;
- situations becoming emotionally charged;
- team culture.

3.1 Opposing objectives

Sometimes you will have a person in your team who just isn't a 'team player', and who is reluctant to accept anything you say without discussion.

When you give an instruction to such a person it is important to communicate clearly and, in most situations, to explain **why** you are giving that particular instruction. Your aim is to achieve:

- a better team spirit;
- a more co-operative attitude;
- better individual performance.

However, you may also be creating a climate in which team members feel that they can query your instructions.

Activity 48

3 mins

Having team members query your instructions has its positive side – but can also have a negative one.

What would you say could be positive about it?

_____

_____

What would you say could be negative about it?

_____

_____

Part of the positive side ought to be obvious: if people don't understand your explanations and instructions, it's good for them to feel able to ask questions. Otherwise they may make expensive mistakes.

Less obviously, perhaps, when people feel free to query instructions they are also more likely to bring problems to your attention on their own initiative.

The negative side is when individual members of the workforce get in the habit of querying the validity of your decisions rather than their own understanding of them. This can undermine your authority and can lead to arguments and bad feeling.

A good first line manager needs to be aware of situations where confrontation is called for, skilled in the techniques of confrontation and assertive enough to use them.

Thus, while it is often a good idea to consult more experienced members of your staff, and perhaps even occasionally to encourage the whole team's participation in reaching certain decisions, you should make sure they understand that, while it's acceptable to query instructions that they don't understand, it's not acceptable for them to query your actual decisions.

You need to 'take your team with you': you can't afford to let an argument arise over every decision you make.

So how can you deal with arguments about, and objections to, your decisions?

Mina told Harriet to reorganize the job estimate files so that there was a separate file for each existing customer, with estimates for potential customers being left in the original 'general' folder. In future, each time a potential customer accepted an estimate, and thus became an 'existing customer', a new file for that customer was to be set up, and all the documentation relating to that customer was to be moved into it.

After three months Mina realised that these new files were not being set up as she had requested, and ticked Harriet off about it. Harriet was unhappy: 'It's a daft idea anyway', she said. 'It means that every time we make a sale to a new customer, I have to scroll right thought the general folder to pull out all the previous estimates we've sent them even the ones they didn't accept. I haven't got time to do that every few days'.

Activity 49

3 mins

Describe what you would say if you were Harriet's manager.

_____

_____

_____

Harriet may well be right that the way Mina asked her to process new customer files was time-consuming, but as a manager, Mina must protect her authority: she can't simply let Harriet get away with it.

However, the answer is not simply to say: 'I'm in charge, do what I say – or else'. Harriet may obey, but she will resent this approach, and the working relationship may be seriously damaged.

Mina should:

- use her communication skills to make sure that Harriet has a full and fair opportunity to give her side of the story;
- take accurate notes.

If the problem is not resolved at this stage but becomes a disciplinary or grievance situation, accurate notes are particularly important, Mina should check the main points with Harriet to make sure that the notes record the situation correctly.

Mina might approach Harriet in the following way.

'You ignored my specific instructions, and that is unacceptable. When I give an instruction I expect it to be carried out. It's not up to you to decide whether to carry it out or not. If you have a problem with something I have asked you to do, say so there and then. I'm always prepared to listen to reasonable suggestions. Now, please get the new files separated out by Thursday. When you have done it, come back and see me, and then we'll discuss whether there's a better way of doing it in future.'

By handling the disagreement this way Mina protects her authority. While accepting that Harriet may have a point, she opens the way to resolving the problem in the future.

3.2 Threatened values

People will be unwilling to compromise if they feel that their values are being threatened. It is often difficult for us to explain precisely what we mean by our 'values', but usually it is things such as telling the truth, being tidy, doing what you say you will do, and so on. If negotiators are able to identify when one or other of the parties feel that their values are being threatened, they are more likely to be able to move the negotiations forward.

3.3 Criticism

A large percentage of the manager's (and negotiator's) time is spent in giving feedback. It is the only way in which other people can measure the impact of their actions.

Feedback can be seen by the person receiving it as either constructive comment or as criticism. If the latter, it is likely to result in conflict. However, if you are careful to use the interpersonal skills we discussed in Session C, then any feedback you give should be received in the right way.

3.4 Roused emotions

Any situation in which emotions are aroused is going to be difficult to handle. This is where transactional analysis (discussed in Session A) can be useful. By appealing to the Adult in the other person you should be able to bring the discussion onto a more neutral, impersonal level, and then explore the problem more calmly.

3.5 Team culture

Negative team culture can make negotiations extremely difficult.

> When Jean took over as first line manager in the training department of a company supplying parts to the armed forces, she found that the members of her team were all ex-military personnel with a strong dislike of taking instructions from a woman.

In such situations there is little that first line managers can do except invoke their position power and try, over time, to use their personal power to win the team over.

4 Resolving conflict situations

There are many ways of handling conflict, from taking formal disciplinary action at one extreme to deciding to ignore the situation at the other. However, as a first line manager it is in your interest to use all the skills you have learned in this workbook to negotiate an outcome that is acceptable to both sides.

You may be personally involved in the conflict or you may have to deal with conflict between two members of your workforce.

4.1 Conflict involving you personally

Jerry was sent over to the warehouse to talk to the packers about new rules for disposing of waste packing materials. The packers, who were a notoriously difficult bunch, shuffled and sniggered through Jerry's five-minute presentation. There were several interruptions to ask deliberately silly questions and Jerry's confidence was badly dented. She finished by saying 'You may think it's a joke, but you'll be laughing on the other side of your faces when Mr Khan does his next inspection'. This was greeted with derision.

Activity 50

3 mins

What was the problem in this situation? What could Jerry have done about it?

_____

_____

The packers were a team, with common values and attitudes. The problem was that their values were negative ones from Jerry's point of view. The packers' culture allowed them to break all the normal rules of politeness in order to make her life difficult. Jerry's own outburst at the end only made things worse. The episode would have damaged her authority, and her attempt to get them to buy into the new disposal procedures would probably have failed.

A team, then, starts out with a strong sense of its identity, position and values, and is capable of maintaining them in the face of outside pressure.

When you are addressing your own team, you should be able to assume that they will have a positive attitude towards you. When you are negotiating with them there should be no major barriers to overcome.

Teams are likely to resist challenges to their accepted beliefs, attitudes and practices.

With an uncommitted or actually hostile team it is different. Even the world's greatest negotiator would have trouble winning them over in five minutes flat. You need to do some work behind the scenes in order to overcome – or at least weaken – some of the barriers.

Activity 51

5 mins

Here are two approaches that Jerry could adopt towards a team with a strongly negative position. Write down what you think of each of them.

'Come on, guys, give me a break. I've had a hard day and I could do without all this aggro.'

_____

_____

'I've come to explain this new procedure to you because Mr Khan has instructed me to. So let's just get it over with, shall we?'

_____

_____

In the first version, Jerry is basically pleading with the packers to be nice to her. In the second she is invoking Mr Khan's authority – passing the buck, in other words. Both are poor approaches because they undermine Jerry's authority and weaken her ability to negotiate.

Here is a model for how Jerry could have approached her task. It is all about influencing the attitude of the packing team.

It is important for Jerry to have the packers' team leader on her side, so she should talk to him beforehand.

She could perhaps ask the team leader to introduce the briefing, thus adding extra credibility to the event. This will ensure that Jerry has at least one sympathetic listener in the audience.

Jerry should identify one of the packers to work on. This person should be an opinion former – a person who has a strong influence on the rest of the team. If this person takes a responsible and positive attitude to health and safety issues, all the better.

She should talk privately to the opinion former and find out how the team is likely to react to the new rules, and the real reasons for their opposition. If she can deal with these problems constructively, she can then ask for advice and invite practical help during the presentation. This should mean a second sympathetic listener.

The next stage is the short briefing itself. Jerry should use the connection she has already made with the team leader and the opinion former by saying things such as:

'Sam's already mentioned to me that you are concerned about. . .'

'. . .and I know Kevin agrees with me. . .'

She can also ask Sam and Kevin to explain or reinforce some points for her. This will help her to convince the team. The logic is that this team doesn't start out with any confidence in Jerry, but does have confidence in Sam and Kevin. Jerry can use this fact to win their acceptance of her message.

4.2 Conflict between other people

When you are having to resolve conflict between other people the chances of success are greatly improved if:

- each side respects the needs and feelings of the other;
- each side tries to understand first, then be understood;
- neither side feels superior or more powerful;
- each side honestly communicates their thoughts and feelings;
- each side participates voluntarily;
- the desired outcome for both sides is to achieve a win-win situation.

The remainder of this session looks at one approach to solving conflict between members of your staff.

5 The 4-step model for resolving conflict

Nearly all conflicts involve underlying emotional issues. The stronger the feelings, the more difficult the resolution. Therefore, to resolve a conflict, it is essential to address the feelings of each side.

The following model for resolving conflict, based on the negotiating model described in Session C, focuses in particular on identifying and understanding emotions.

Step 1 Seek to understand

Remember to focus on the feelings behind the behaviour rather than the behaviour itself.

- Get each side to reveal their true feelings.
- Confirm that they are committed to solving the problem.
- Seek to understand the causes of each side's feelings.
- Summarize what you have understood.
- Find out what the underlying emotional needs are that are not being met.
- Check that each side has heard the other side's feelings about the conflict – and understood them.
- Show empathy.
- Ask: What would help them feel better?

Step 2 Clarify the objectives

- Decide what your main objective is in seeking a solution.

Step 3 Explore the options

- Encourage as many suggestions for solutions as possible (without evaluating them).
- Discuss each side's feelings about each option.
- Consider the implications of each option.

Step 4 Agree a solution

- Choose a final solution which optimises positive feelings and minimizes negative feelings.

Activity 52

EXTENSION 7
You might like to read chapter 4 of Roger Bennett's book *Personal Effectiveness*. It focuses on managing a team and suggests ways of handling conflict.

You are a first line manager for Creative Images Ltd, which is a medium-sized company in the advertising industry. Peter Naven and Graham Sansom are two experienced members of your work team. Unfortunately they just don't seem to be able to work together and are continually bickering and arguing. You notice that they frequently accuse each other of interfering with each other's work. In fact they are so unco-operative towards each other that their behaviour is affecting the performance of the whole team.

What is the first step you should take to deal with this situation?

You may have said one of the following.

- 'Have them both in my office and talk to them about it'.
- 'Find out what's going on.'
- 'Try to discover what's behind the problem.'

These are all sensible answers to give. The first step is obviously to **find out the facts** and make sure they understand each other's point of view.

Activity 53

5 mins

What sort of information would you want to find out from Peter and Graham?

_____

_____

_____

_____

You might have suggested the following.

- How does each of them see the problem?
- How long have they been working together, and when did the trouble first start?
- Is there any personal problem between them outside work?
- How well defined are the jobs done by Peter and Graham?

The aim at this stage is to collect all the evidence without prejudging the outcome. When you think you have gathered all the facts you can move on to the next step, **clarifying your objectives**.

Activity 54 · 3 mins

Tick one of the following to indicate what will be your main objective in trying to resolve the conflict between Peter and Graham.

To resolve the matter at all costs ☐

To get the team's performance back to full efficiency ☐

To get Peter and Graham to be friends ☐

To discipline them ☐

To adopt the objective of resolving the matter at all costs may mean that you have to be prepared to dismiss the two staff members. If you aim to get them to be friends, you may have set yourself an impossible task. Alternatively, deciding to discipline Peter and Graham is prejudging the issue. The most important priority for you as first line manager is achievement of the task. Your main objective, therefore, is likely to be 'To get the team's performance back to full efficiency'.

The next step is to **explore the options**.

Activity 55 · 3 mins

You now know certain facts relating to the problem between Peter and Graham. These are as follows.

■ They have worked together in the past.
■ The disagreements are entirely about job responsibilities and whose job it is to do what.
■ You value the technical skills and creative output of both men.

Suggest two possible solutions that will achieve your objective of getting the team's performance back to full efficiency.

It is important for you to keep your main objective in mind when looking at alternative solutions. You may have suggested some of the following options.

- Redefine and clarify Peter and Graham's job descriptions.
- Move one of them into another team so they don't have to work together.
- Reorganize the two jobs so that there's clearly no overlap of responsibilities.
- Confront Peter and Graham and challenge their behaviour.
- Meet with both of them. Explain the impact of their behaviour on the rest of the staff and offer to help them talk through the problem together to try to resolve any differences.

Once you have identified a number of options, the next step is to choose the best one to meet your main objective. Choosing the best option isn't always easy. The secret is to go through each course of action and work out the likely result of selecting that option.

The sorts of questions you need to ask here are as follows.

- How will this option work out?
- What will be the overall effect on the team?
- How far will this solution go towards meeting my objective?
- What are the costs (financial and otherwise) of taking this action?
- Will I be satisfied with the outcome?
- Will it solve the problem in the long term?
- What new problems might it give rise to?

Activity 56 · 5 mins

One of the proposed solutions to your problem was to move either Peter or Graham to another team so they don't have to work together. Now look ahead and try to work out the possible results of taking this action.

_____

_____

_____

You may have suggested some of these possible outcomes.

- Your team may lose technical or creative skills, which can't easily be replaced.
- You may have to retrain other staff members to fill any gaps resulting from Peter or Graham's departure.
- Arguments may flare up again whenever the two come into contact with each other because their dispute has never been resolved.
- The problem may be resolved.

After you have worked out the implications of all the options in the same way, you are ready to choose a solution. You need to involve both Peter and Graham in this last step because there may still be factors (feelings, other causes of conflict) that you have missed in earlier stages.

But once the solution is reached, it must be made clear that your decision is final and no further arguments will be considered.

6 Achieving a win-win situation

Activity 57

3 mins

Highlight the square in this matrix which should represent the best outcome of a negotiation.

	Win	Lose
Win	Win - Win	Win - Lose
Lose	Lose - Win	Lose - Lose

It may seem tempting for one side to win and the other to lose, but this often proves counter-productive because:

- if one side has clearly 'lost the argument' it may be repudiated by more senior people on that side;
- a losing negotiator may feel resentful, and may seek revenge at some later date.

The best outcome is where both sides perceive themselves as winning.

Naturally, a result in which **neither** side wins is an outright failure.

Self-assessment 4

12 mins

1 You can influence action on a decision most successfully by using your

_____ .

2 People will be unwilling to compromise if they feel that their _____ are being threatened.

3 The chances of resolving a conflict are greatly improved if each side respects

the _____ and _____ of the other.

4 Suggest two reasons for explaining to your team **why** you are giving that particular instruction.

_____

_____

5 What three actions are involved in step 3 of the conflict resolution model?

_____

_____

_____

Answers to these questions can be found on page 116.

7 Summary

- As a first line manager you have three kinds of power:

  - position power;
  - expert power;
  - personal power.

- When disagreements arise, you should protect your power while accepting any valid points that the other person has to make.

- You should only use disciplinary procedures as a very last resort. It's far better to use persuasion and encouragement whenever possible.

- The main causes of conflict are:

  - opposing objectives;
  - values being threatened;
  - feedback being taken as criticism;
  - situations becoming emotionally charged;
  - team culture.

- The four steps in resolving conflict are:

  - seek to understand;
  - clarify the objectives;
  - explore the options;
  - agree a solution.

- You must always use your power for the good of the team and to further its defined tasks.

Performance checks

1 Quick quiz

Question 1 By learning to recognize the habitual _____ among your team, you can help them to change their unproductive behaviours, to uncross their wires and improve communication and _____.

Question 2 Which type of organizational relationship is involved where a manager or team leader reports to two or more senior managers for different purposes?

Question 3 What are the **three** ways in which an organization's culture may be oriented?

_____

_____

Question 4 Identify **four** of the important personal qualities needed by a good first line manager.

_____

_____

_____

_____

Question 5 How would you define the word integrity?

_____

Question 6 What is the task of the person who plays the role of Mediator in a team?

_____

Performance checks

Question 7 A team will only be really effective if you, as the leader, are able to:

■ allocate the team members to the roles that best suit their _____

and _____;

■ develop a culture of _____, respect and mutual support within

the group.

Question 8 How would you define 'empathy'?

_____

Question 9 Suggest two benefits to a manager of using humour.

_____

_____

Question 10 According to the concept of _____ _____, people who
are best at getting in touch with their own and other people's emotions are
more successful both at work and in their social lives.

Question 11 Suggest two reasons why it is a good idea to sit at 90 degrees to a person
during a one-to-one meeting.

_____

_____

Question 12 Research shows that 7% of communication is through what you have to

_____. Of the other 93%, 55% is communicated through the way

you _____ and 38% through the way you _____.

Question 13 In negotiations, what do we mean by the 'negotiable area'?

_____

_____

Question 14 The chances of achieving success in negotiations are greatly improved if each

side honestly communicates their _____ and _____.

Question 15 Give two reasons why it is not a good idea for one side to win a dispute
outright and the other to lose.

_____

_____

Answers to these questions can be found on pages 118–119.

2 Workbook assessment

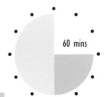

60 mins

Jack Taylor has recently been appointed manager of a team of ten in a large firm of travel agents. The team comprises eight holiday bookings staff, one administrative assistant and one technical assistant responsible for maintenance of the computer system.

Until his appointment, Jack worked for 15 years as a holiday bookings assistant at another location within the company. Sarah Price, an experienced member of his new team, had expected to be appointed and is very resentful of Jack's appointment. She feels that she has more local knowledge than Jack and gets on well with most of the team.

The company operates an on-line booking system and operational decisions often have to be made very quickly. In addition, Jack's line manager has asked him to look at developing new procedures for staff training and improving the response rate to queries from customers. Many members of staff have been complaining that they are under too much stress already and can't work any faster.

Write down your answers to the following questions.

- What problems is Jack likely to encounter in establishing his authority within the team?
- How can he most effectively establish his authority to get the best from his staff?
- What should Jack's approach be to managing the team in order to bring in the changes required by the senior management?
- How should Jack handle the negative attitude shown by Sarah Price?

Your answer to this assignment will probably be about two pages.

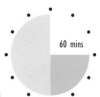

3 Work-based assignment

60 mins

S/NVQ C1.1, C4.3

The time guide for this assignment gives you an idea of how long it is likely to take you to write up your findings. You will find that you need to spend some additional time gathering information, perhaps talking to colleagues and thinking about the assignment.

Your response to this assignment may form useful evidence for your S/NVQ portfolio. The assignment is designed to help you demonstrate:

- your ability to act assertively;
- your ability to communicate;
- your ability to manage yourself;
- your ability to influence others.

What you should do

Think of a particularly difficult dispute that you have had to deal with at work in the past. It should involve a situation that caused problems between members of your staff.

Describe the specific nature of the conflict, its causes and the individuals involved. There may be documents that you can refer to which will give a background to the problem.

You may also need to interview the staff members involved to get their reaction to how you handled the situation. This may be sensitive, so you will need to use your judgement as to whether interviews are appropriate.

Then answer the following questions about the way you resolved the conflict.

- What impact did it have on the team and their ability to complete their team objectives?
- To what extent did you use your personal rather than position power when negotiating a resolution?
- Did you encounter any specific difficulties in dealing with people that you felt inadequate to deal with?
- Did you use the 4-step model for resolving conflict in this situation? If so, give details and describe how successful it was.

■ How did you ensure that the parties to the dispute were satisfied with your decision?

You should record your findings, and then try to decide what you can deduce from the information you have collected. Your overall aim in this assignment is to answer the following questions.

■ What have I discovered about how successful my negotiating was in this situation?
■ Did I fully involve the parties to the dispute? How do they feel about my performance and the way I used my authority?
■ How will this knowledge lead me to manage my team more effectively in the future?

What you should write

Present your findings in a structured way using appropriate sub-headings.

Add to your findings a list of key pointers that are relevant to your future negotiating activities.

Reflect and review

1 Reflect and review

Now that you have completed your work on managing relationships at work, let's review the workbook objectives. The first objective was:

■ to describe the types of structure which form the basis of relationships in organizations.

You should understand the effect of different structures on the way the organization functions, and the way in which some can be static and others change according to the needs of the work. You should also appreciate the importance of developing formal and informal relationships both inside and outside your organization.

You may want to ask yourself the following questions.

■ Do I make the best use of the relationships that I have developed?

_____

_____

_____

■ Are there any other ways in which I could develop relationships which could make my work more effective?

_____

_____

_____

The second workbook objective was:

■ to develop qualities and skills that will promote positive team relationships.

Behaviour breeds behaviour. By developing certain ways of behaving you can promote harmony in your team and encourage them to adopt working practices which benefit both the workforce and the organization. Things to think about include the following.

■ How far does my own behaviour reflect the interpersonal skills and attributes needed by an effective team leader?

_____

_____

_____

■ What practical steps can I take to change my own and my staff's behaviour in order to strengthen team cohesion?

_____

_____

_____

The next objective was:

■ to be able to apply the principles of influence and persuasion to achieve objectives.

There are a number of factors of influence which will affect one or other side in a negotiation and you can use these to strengthen your bargaining position. You should also recognize those factors that might influence you in a negotiating situation. Means of persuasion include verbal and non-verbal techniques.

Points to think about include the following.

■ Which factors of influence can I use to advantage when dealing with my staff or with other people inside and outside the organization?

_____

_____

_____

■ What strategies can I adopt to improve my powers of persuasion?

_____

_____

_____

The last objective was:

■ to use appropriate techniques to resolve conflict.

There are many reasons why conflict might result in disruption in the workplace. It is the first line manager's responsibility to identify sources of conflict and use the skills of persuasion and negotiation to get each party to agree to a compromise. You may want to think about the following points.

■ How is conflict currently dealt with in my work team?

_____

_____

_____

■ In future, how will I make myself aware of conflict situations when they arise, and how will I ensure that it is resolved in a win-win way?

_____

_____

_____

2 Action plan

Use this plan to further develop for yourself a course of action you want to take. Make a note in the left-hand column of the issues or problems you want to tackle, and then decide what you want to do, and make a note in column 2.

The resources you need might include time, materials, information or money. You may need to negotiate for some of them, but others could be easy to acquire, like half an hour of somebody's time, or a chapter of a book. Put whatever you need in column 3. No plan means anything without a timescale, so put a realistic target completion date in column 4.

Desired outcomes			
1 Issues	2 Action	3 Resources	4 Target completion
Actual outcomes			

3 Extensions

Extension 1

Book	*Improve Your People Skills*
Author	Peter Honey
Edition	Second edition
Publisher	CIPD

Extension 2

Book	*The New Manager*
Author	Mike Woods
Edition	1994
Publisher	Element Books

Extension 3

Book	*Negotiating Persuading and Influencing*
Author	Alan Fowler
Edition	2000
Publisher	CIPD

Extension 4

Book	*How to be Twice as Smart*
Author	Scott Witt
Edition	1993
Publisher	Reward Books

Extension 5

Book	*Introducing NLP*
Author	Sue Knight
Edition	1999
Publisher	CIPD

Extension 6

Book	*How to Communicate Effectively*
Author	Bert Decker
Edition	1990
Publisher	Kogan Page

Extension 7

Book	*Personal Effectiveness*
Author	Roger Bennett
Edition	1994
Publisher	Kogan Page

4 Answers to self-assessment questions

**Self-assessment 1
on page 17**

1 The relationships are as follows.

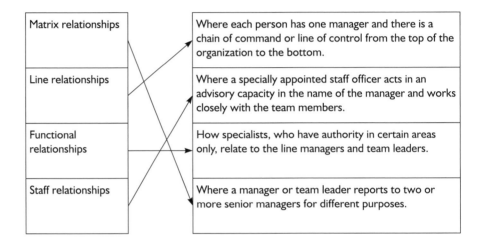

Matrix relationships	Where each person has one manager and there is a chain of command or line of control from the top of the organization to the bottom.
Line relationships	Where a specially appointed staff officer acts in an advisory capacity in the name of the manager and works closely with the team members.
Functional relationships	How specialists, who have authority in certain areas only, relate to the line managers and team leaders.
Staff relationships	Where a manager or team leader reports to two or more senior managers for different purposes.

2 Two ways in which you can develop informal relationships at work are through sports and social activities, and through getting to know people at meetings.

3 Problems associated with liasing with external experts include the fact that lines of authority may be blurred and other members of the team may find it difficult to accept and implement their proposals.

4 The three ego-states in transactional analysis are Parent, Adult and Child.

5 An understanding of the principles of **TRANSACTIONAL ANALYSIS** can help you to manage the **RELATIONSHIPS** between you and your team and between different members of the team.

6

Parent	**Adult**	**Child**
Protective Authoritarian Critical	Unemotional Calculating	Spontaneous Fun-loving Manipulative

Self-assessment 2 on page 50

1   Behaviour breeds **BEHAVIOUR**.

2   The five roles in a strong team are Achiever, Provocateur, Consolidator, Reflector and Mediator.

3   First line managers who want **LOYALTY** from the team must be **LOYAL** in return.

4   First line managers who show **INTEGRITY** get respect.

5   A first line manager needs to be **FIRM** in putting the achievement of the team's objectives above everything else.

6   Taking an **INTEREST** in members of the workforce is arguably the most important job a first line manager has to do in his/her role as **TEAM LEADER**.

7   The seven interpersonal skills that we looked at in the workbook, and that are generally agreed to be the most important for a first line manager are: ability to inspire, openness, empathy, firmness, flexibility, humour and interest in people.

Self-assessment 3 on page 80

1   The correct answers are as follows.

   a   'Prepare this order for Mentrim Ltd, would you?'   REQUEST
   b   'Don't argue, just do it!'   ORDER
   c   'Please do your best to get this done on time. It's for the   PLEA
       good of the whole team, you know!'
   d   'Can you just adjust this so that the legs don't protrude?   REQUEST
       Thanks.'

2   The best advice is (b), when you would try to find out whether your instructions were clear. A simple misunderstanding might be the reason why the team members haven't carried out the task.

3   Expert knowledge is particularly valuable if you are suffering under the negative influences of weak position power or poor personal relationships.

4   You can boost someone's self-esteem by:

   ■ making them believe that they have a reputation to live up to;
   ■ making them feel needed;
   ■ asking questions that make them feel knowledgeable;
   ■ making them feel that there is a challenge to be met.

5   You can use neuro-linguistic programming to build a **RAPPORT** with someone.

6 The six ways in which which you can use non-verbal communication are through your eyes, facial expression, voice, gestures, posture and appearance.

7 If one side clearly loses in a negotiation, the risks are that:

a someone more senior on the other side may repudiate the agreement;
b the losing negotiator may feel resentful and seek revenge at a later date.

8 The six steps in negotiation are:

1 preparation;
2 exchange of initial views;
3 exploring possible solutions;
4 identifying common ground;
5 reaching a compromise;
6 implementing the compromise.

Self-assessment 4 on page 100

1 You can influence action on a decision most successfully by using your **PERSONAL POWER**.

2 People will be unwilling to compromise if they feel that their **VALUES** are being threatened.

3 The chances of resolving a conflict are greatly improved if each side respects the **NEEDS** and **FEELINGS** of the other.

4 Reasons for explaining to your team **why** you are giving that particular instruction are that it will result in:

■ a better team spirit;
■ a more co-operative attitude;
■ better individual performance.

5 The three actions involved in step 3 of the conflict resolution model are:
■ encourage as many suggestions for solutions as possible;
■ discuss each side's feelings about each option;
■ consider the implications of each option.

5 Answers to activities

Activity 9 on page 14

Your answer should have been as follows.

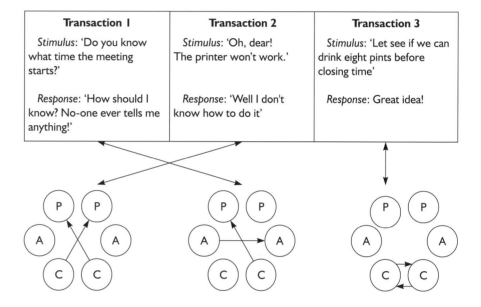

Transaction 1	Transaction 2	Transaction 3
Stimulus: 'Do you know what time the meeting starts?'	*Stimulus*: 'Oh, dear! The printer won't work.'	*Stimulus*: 'Let see if we can drink eight pints before closing time'
Response: 'How should I know? No-one ever tells me anything!'	*Response*: 'Well I don't know how to do it'	*Response*: Great idea!

Activity 25 on page 44

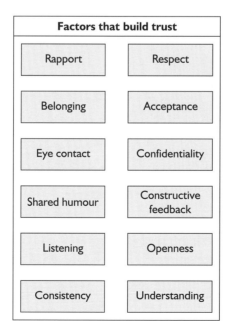

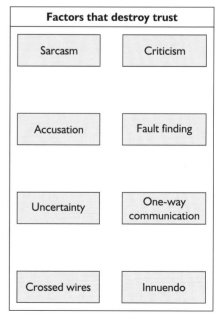

Factors that build trust

Rapport, Respect, Belonging, Acceptance, Eye contact, Confidentiality, Shared humour, Constructive feedback, Listening, Openness, Consistency, Understanding

Factors that destroy trust

Sarcasm, Criticism, Accusation, Fault finding, Uncertainty, One-way communication, Crossed wires, Innuendo

6 Answers to the quick quiz

Answer 1 By learning to recognize the habitual **BEHAVIOURS** among your staff, you can help them to change their unproductive behaviours, uncross their wires and improve communication and **UNDERSTANDING**.

Answer 2 The organizational relationship where a manager or team leader reports to two or more senior managers for different purposes is a matrix relationship.

Answer 3 An organization's culture may be profit-oriented, systems-oriented or people-oriented.

Answer 4 Personal qualities you could have chosen include:

- loyalty;
- integrity;
- fairness;
- determination;
- dependability.

Answer 5 Integrity means sticking to your principles and being honest and consistent.

Answer 6 The task of the Mediator is to keep a harmonious atmosphere and resolve conflict within the team.

Answer 7 A team will only be really effective if you, as the leader, are able to:

- allocate the team members to the roles that best suit their **SKILLS** and **COMPETENCIES**;
- develop a culture of **TRUST**, respect and mutual support within the group.

Answer 8 Empathy involves relating to and showing sensitivity towards others.

Answer 9 By using humour you:

- encourage people to listen more closely;
- help them to learn;
- make you appear more human;
- make people feel that they belong to a good team;
- motivate them to make an extra effort.

Answer 10   According to the concept of **EMOTIONAL INTELLIGENCE**, people who are best at getting in touch with their own and other people's emotions are more successful both at work and in their social lives.

Answer 11   Sitting at 90 degrees enables you to have eye contact and is not confrontational.

Answer 12   Research shows that 7% of communication is through what you have to **SAY**. Of the other 93%, 55% is communicated through the way you **LOOK** and 38% through the way you **ACT**.

Answer 13   In negotiations, the 'negotiable area' is the area where the maximum and minimum positions of the two sides overlap, and where agreement will eventually be reached.

Answer 14   The chances of achieving success in negotiations are greatly improved if each side honestly communicates their **THOUGHTS** and **FEELINGS**.

Answer 15   It is not a good idea for one side to win a dispute outright and the other to lose because:

- if one side has clearly 'lost the argument' it may be repudiated by more senior people on that side;
- a losing negotiator may feel resentful, and may seek revenge at some later date.

7 Certificate

Completion of this certificate by an authorized person shows that you have worked through all the parts of this workbook and satisfactorily completed the assessments. The certificate provides a record of what you have done that may be used for exemptions or as evidence of prior learning against other nationally certificated qualifications.

Pergamon Flexible Learning and ILM are always keen to refine and improve their products. One of the key sources of information to help this process are people who have just used the product. If you have any information or views, good or bad, please pass these on.

INSTITUTE OF LEADERSHIP & MANAGEMENT
SUPER SERIES

Managing Relationships at Work

....

has satisfactorily completed this workbook

Name of signatory ....

Position ....

Signature ....

Date ....

Official stamp

Fourth Edition

INSTITUTE OF LEADERSHIP & MANAGEMENT
SUPERSERIES
FOURTH EDITION